ANGLE
RECRUITING

How to Hire the Right People
for Your Sales Organization

FULVIO FELLETTI

Published by Fellettis 2016

Copyright © 2015 Fulvio Felletti

www.fellettis.com
You can contact the author at: book@fellettis.com

Disclaimer
Every effort has been made to ensure that this book is free from error or omissions. Information provided is of general nature only and should not be considered legal or financial advice. The intent is to offer a variety of information to the reader. However, the author, publisher, editor or their agents or representatives shall not accept responsibility for any loss or inconvenience caused to a person or organisation relying on this information.

Book cover design and formatting services by BookCoverCafe.com

ISBN: 978-981-09-7868-6 (pbk)

         978-981-09-7869-3 (e-bk)

To my wonderful wife for all her love, support and patience.
And to my loving parents who have always believed in me.

TABLE OF CONTENTS

FOREWORD

The digitalisation revolution is now well underway, with new businesses and products/services materialising almost daily (and dis-intermediating incumbents) and older businesses dissolving or being absorbed by 'disrupters' more rapidly. Other 'traditional' enterprises are experiencing rapidly shifting paradigms (especially customer expectations) within their markets. The ability to adapt rapidly to changing environments and customer demands will be an increasingly critical path for all enterprises. Businesses have confronted similar transformations in the past, but the current difference is in the speed of change, the emergence of disruptive forces across many industries and a re-valuation of companies' 'digital' potential. The latter point has not been lost on senior executives, investors and boards of directors, who now have even shorter time horizons to realise a return on invested capital. This is fomenting some of the highest financial churning (mergers and acquisitions; corporate restructurings; downsizings; bankruptcies; etc.) in history.

In this new world, hiring the 'right' employees, especially sales executives, managers and field/inside salespeople, is becoming even more crucial, and will require leaders to become particularly astute at recognising the appropriate talent for their organisations. This requires a new, bolder, more structured approach to matching the requisite enterprise skill sets with those exhibited (or potentially manifested) by applicants based on specific, repeatable (though also flexible) criteria, models and frameworks. And, it will demand that recruiting personnel become even more sensitive to the nuances of different generations' (X, Y and Z, boomers and millennials) workplace aspirations and requirements.

Moreover, this new environment will demand that virtually all enterprises become more engaged with their prospects and clients via multiple (digital, physical, etc.) channels. This (more) service-oriented approach is already underway, with many companies now offering various products 'as a service', to secure longer-term, deeper customer support relationships. This move from selling 'products' to providing 'digital services' is also being driven by content and subscription offerings that are more virtual or informational (think Apple or Android app stores, or Facebook's social network 'connectedness').Indeed, the value of these companies is increasingly in the 'digital personas' of their customers that they are able to create, curate and monetise.

All participants in this new world will require 'digital' skills and different mindsets, but for client-facing employees, especially sales executives, this change will be most profound. With a higher proportion of product and service sales being executed 'virtually' (i.e., via the Internet and world-wide web), 21st-century sales executives must incorporate new customer support models that ensure higher engagement levels. In some ways, this paradigm shift is analogous to one that IBM successfully employed in the 1960s and '70s,when it sold and maintained its mainframe computers, complete with software and peripherals, as well as services, via highly trained 'service engineers' (SE). These SEs typically had engineering degrees and acted as advocates and 'advisers', ensuring that their customers' IT infrastructures were well maintained, met expectations and were upgraded as necessary.

While the specific skills have changed, many of the 21st-century product/service models (e.g., X as a service) are similar, and their support philosophies and disciplines bear a remarkable resemblance to IBM's 50-plus-year-old approach. Thus, to complement ubiquitous online marketing approaches, digital world sales models will thus demand more sophisticated communications skills, deeper content (product and service) knowledge, better financial (e.g., income statement and balance sheet) acumen, the ability to explain and highlight successful case examples, and the skill to build trust-based 'consigliore' relationships. The latter is one of the more important categories, and one emphasised throughout this book. In fact, 21st-century sales executives are increasingly becoming part of the overall value delivery chain, in that they become a more intrinsic part of the ongoing product/service relationship (i.e., more overlap between sales and customer support) renewal, driving a 'customer lifetime value' mentality. This is a skill emphasised in many chapters of this book—from the onset of the sales recruiting process through final selection, then as part of advanced training and techniques for ongoing development.

In his discussion of the Angle Recruiting model, Mr. Felletti takes an engineering (four-stage) approach to a more holistic, cross-cultural and cross-generational sales recruiting process that can be utilised to attract millennials, as well as generations X, Y and Z candidates from across the globe (it can also be applied to hiring other professionals).He also highlights and explains some of the newer criteria that should be part of any sales organisation's ongoing evolution and development process. The Angle Recruiting model emphasises the use of: compelling job descriptions; great sourcing; comprehensive interviewing; and a 'scientific' or architected selection and onboarding process. It also highlights the need to exploit new and existing models/ frameworks (like value selling, etc.) to achieve these goals and retain the next generation of sales executives.

Beyond some excellent philosophical constructs and ideas, *Angle Recruiting* provides a practical guide (as well as 'cookbook' processes and helpful checklists) for recognising, hiring and training the next generation of sales leaders and practitioners. This disciplined approach and the models and adaptations it engenders should be required reading for all senior and mid-level executives involved in the sales recruiting, hiring, management and 'upskilling' processes.

Dale Kutnick
SVP Emeritus & Distinguished Analyst
Gartner, Inc.

INTRODUCTION

The growing presence of millennials in the workforce requires that employers adapt to the lessons learnt in recruitment over the past few decades. Many of today's most desirable candidates approach the job market in ways that pose a serious challenge to those who cling to outdated approaches to recruiting. Society has changed, and with it the workplace. This book will help you adapt to these changes; it will give you the tools you need to bring precisely the kind of people on board that will be best equipped to address today's most coveted customer demographics in powerful and persuasive ways.

In what follows, we'll look closely at the changing environment for sales organisations (this means looking at millennials both as employees and as customers). It is important to understand the specific ways that Generation Y and Generation Z (soon to shape the market in their own way) are different from the generations (the Xers and the boomers) that preceded them. The recruiting approach I will advocate in this book depends upon a nuanced understanding of these tidal shifts, so we'll explore these ideas in detail before moving on to the strategies you'll need to apply to source and interview candidates effectively in the 21st century.

Once we've got our feet beneath us (i.e., once we understand precisely where we stand), we'll turn to Angle Recruiting, a revolutionary and proven four-stage approach to recruiting that has been tailor-made to help organisations adapt to and grow in today's business climate. The four stages are: 1) writing the perfect job description; 2) sourcing to get the most out of the 21st century talent pool; 3) interviewing; and 4) selecting and onboarding.

In the third section of this book, each of the four stages will be covered in turn. My extensive experience with the recruiting process has taught me that the interviewing stage is the one that is the most difficult to get right. The insights contained in the chapters on interviewing are, therefore, the beating heart at the centre of Angle Recruiting. The chapter on the interviewing stage contains a powerful and proven five-step approach to candidate interviews. These five steps make up the Angle Framework. I'll introduce these steps here:

1. **Define Your Organisation and its Needs** – The first step in the process is to understand your company's unique DNA. Just as it is crucial to understand the market in which you are operating, it is also undeniably important to

understand what your organisation needs—not all organisations' needs are identical, so taking a firm grasp of your organisational DNA and its needs (we do this so we can better define an ideal candidate) make up the crucial first step of the interviewing process.

2. **You Now** – The second step is about honestly assessing candidates as they are in the present. I have identified four characteristics (the Big Four) that today's employers should expect from candidates: clear purpose, clock speed, curiosity and competitiveness.

3. **You Tomorrow** – Effective recruiting takes into account not only the present but the future as well. While a candidate might currently dovetail neatly with the organisation's needs, he or she will also need to represent a good fit with the organisation's direction. Though the candidate and the organisation might both be standing at the same crossroads, the candidate's five-year plan might see them taking a different path to the one you have in mind for them and for the organisation.

4. **Plan** – Once you are sure that the candidate will find the path they will walk with the organisation,

a suitable one for both their present and future selves, it will be time to move on to planning, which will involve realistic yet ambitious goal-setting on both the organisation's and the candidate's part. Again, it is crucial that the candidate's plans and the organisation's plans for the candidate intermesh neatly.

5. **Match** – While each of the four steps above focus on asking the right questions (and getting the right answers), the final step sees you give the candidate a chance to control the conversation. Let them speak freely about what they have gleaned from the interviews and also about how they see themselves fitting into the organisation (a three-year outlook is usually enough of a guideline, but the more forward-looking the candidate at this point, the better).

By applying this five-step method to your interviewing methodology you'll not only make your organisation stronger in the present; you'll also be building a future-proof organisation, one that is prepared to cope with further market disruptions (rather than one scrambling to keep up with yesterday's changes).

Why Angle?

I believe that the world could be a better place if only we could match people to the right jobs in the right companies. We could have a world in which people are inspired to achieve their dreams fearlessly; people could go to work with the knowledge (a knowledge that resonates with the desires of the heart) that they are a part of something meaningful and that they are contributing to that meaning; people could be working with people who inspire them, and they can, in turn, inspire those around them. When our job is aligned with our personal drivers, the path to our personal goals is not only shorter, it's also one we enjoy walking—we look forward to the destination, but the journey is sweet as well.

By matching the right people to the right positions and the right organisations we can avoid making capable and driven individuals feel as though they're wasting valuable time in the pursuit of mediocrity. For employers, Angle Recruiting represents a chance to build or grow an organisation based on principles that will guarantee that performance and commitment to organisational goals will reach record levels. Great business results, after all, are the result of alignment between the organisation's goals and those of its employees. A powerful recruiting strategy (and particularly the one you'll find in this book) can align your organisation in this purposeful way.

Purposeful people (those who act with clarity and purpose) tend to be more fulfilled, happier, and more successful. Start to seek out and recruit purposeful people—you'll be given the skills to do so later on—and you'll notice a number of changes in your organisation: employees raise the bar for themselves, each other, and the organisation every day; employees collaborate with each other; they move beyond the not-in-my-backyard syndrome(the mindset that expects sacrifice to be anywhere but in one's own department);they proactively involve their leaders, making them powerful allies in their drive to succeed and close productivity-sapping gaps. Ultimately, money is no longer the main driver in the working relationship, and a lot of the important intangibles start shaping both the working relationship and the organisation-wide culture. Expected (or better-than-expected) results become a matter of course, and nobody rests on their laurels. Your organisation is now a lot more resilient, able to face a volatile world and all of its uncertainty, complexity and ambiguity.

While this book is in no way the first to offer a secret formula that will lead to a more successful and fulfilling organisation, all of the formulae I have encountered in my wide-reaching research and experience lack a key element. Whether it's a focus on management and their leadership skills, on corporate culture and its ability to inspire, or even a focus on interior design (these last authors often make the unsupportable claim that a cosmetic makeover is somehow enough to inspire and motivate employees), all of these theories ignore the necessary three-way match between the individual, the organisation, and their role within it. I cannot understate the importance of this alignment, and the process begins with attracting and hiring the right people. I'm going to show you how to do just that.

To borrow a principle from Rhonda Byrne's powerful books, the energy flows where the focus goes. If you are ready to transform your organisation, bring all of your focus to bear on the recruitment tools you'll find on these pages. You'll find the effort will lead you to powerful, transformative results. Your organisation will become a magnet for truly motivated people who deliver outstanding results for the organisation and its customers. Those who work in this kind of organisation wake up every morning excited about their work; they work hand-in-hand with likeminded people, all of whom are driven by the same passion to act and work in purposeful, achievement-driven ways.

The more you apply powerful recruiting tools, the more you'll create this kind of uniform approach to excellence (i.e., a workplace in which peers share the load and go the extra mile to help each other and the organisation). This goes all the way from the top of the organisation to the bottom.

In time, when individual goals become realised, the belief that no business goal is out of reach will pervade the organisation. Resourcefulness is embedded in every member of the team, and nobody is concerned about availability of resources. Everyone is both a mentor and a mentee; leaders are not dictators – they are coaches. Throughout the organisation, people are proud of their accomplishments and accountable for their mistakes.

The risks of maintaining the status quo

Not too long ago, I was in Hong Kong. I had some time to kill before my scheduled meeting (high up in one of the city's many futuristic and tall buildings), so I decided to do some people-watching in the cafeteria. I sipped on my coffee and watched people file past me and onto one of the escalators that connected the cafeteria with the lobby.

Something immediately grabbed my attention. The vast majority of faces, whether Indian, Chinese, Arab or Caucasian, wore an identical expression. They all wore a grey look; their expressions made it seem as though something positively dreadful was awaiting them at the top of that escalator. Viewed as something of an informal employee survey, the results couldn't have been worse.

It looked as though each and every person who filed past me was starting his or her day with the expectation of more of the same – more starting over, more emotionally unrewarding and unexciting work, merely a series of routine activities utterly divorced from their deepest desires. I wondered how many of the organisations that I saw represented were enjoying record profits that year (probably not many).

The more I thought about it, the more it became evident that ennui and purposelessness were acting like viruses that were spreading from employee to employee. This realisation was a turning point in my life: something just wasn't right with the 21st-century workplace, and that something (like the viruses) needed an antidote.

As a member of a large sales organisation, I had experienced how vital a positive mindset was to success; it meant that one could reflect and magnify positive energy to warm up clients and partners and make them more receptive. Few (next to none) achieve greatness when a pessimistic attitude tethers them firmly to terra firma. Unhappy people suck all the oxygen out of a room; normally positive people (even great ones) can't help but be affected by the grey cloud. In this cloud's shadow, entire teams underperform and so, in the long run, does the organisation.

As I thought more about the problem, I became convinced that I saw a way out of the mire. This journey started with a transformative journey of self-discovery, and

I soon established a not-for-profit organisation focused on supporting people in this journey. Since I refused to let my day-to-day work suffer, my days were incredibly busy, but I was on a mission to change the world one person at a time, and no matter what the sacrifice was to be, I knew deep in my heart that it would be worth it.

As I began talking to more and more people who were infected with the ennui and purposelessness viruses, I saw patterns beginning to develop: the same mistakes, the same domino effect triggered by those mistakes, the same damaged careers, the same sub-par performance, the same tarnished brands. The intentions were there (or had been there once), but the results were lacking; the mind was willing, the flesh weak.

Many of the people I worked with who worked in sales organisations spoke about starting with enthusiasm but finding that enthusiasm wane (often much more quickly than they had expected it to). With each passing day, it became more and more apparent that what was needed was a focus on recruiting, retaining and leading that would lead, not only to higher levels of performance, but also to more fulfilled and (in the simplest terms) happier employees – the connection between these two has been well documented. Just as one person's unhappiness, low energy levels and negative body language trigger similar behaviours in others, so too do motivated, energised, and overtly confident people affect those around them in untold positive ways.

The costs of maintaining the status quo are measurable. According to many observers, lack of motivation at work is costing companies globally several billion dollars in lost productivity. Attrition rates are too high and the employer's brand suffers as a result. In a study published in 2014, Professor Stephen Bevan from The Work Foundation in the UK estimated the cost of absenteeism (largely driven by a lack of motivation)to be around £13 billion per annum. In a Gallup study from the year before, researchers found that the annual cost of lost productivity due to absenteeism was US$40 billion per annum. The issue is not only a matter of perception; it carries with it financial costs that should not—indeed, cannot—be ignored.

Is there something actionable and impactful that people can do to ensure a happier and more productive workforce? Yes, there is, and it starts with putting employees' motivation and personal goals at the very centre of the recruiting process.

PART 1

The Landscape

CHAPTER 1:
A SHIFTING LANDSCAPE

I remember brainstorming in 2007 with my industry peers on how to leverage the new wave of social media platforms like Skype, LinkedIn and Facebook that were becoming more and more popular with each passing day. At that time, we were still leveraging databases like Factiva, D&B and Who's Who to search for leads. In the last decade or so, the generation born after 1980 (Generation Y or the millennials) started entering the job market. As a markedly different class of professionals, they began almost immediately to cause something of a seismic shift in how organisations were approaching and mining the talent pool.

In her bestselling book, *Smart Selling on the Phone and Online*, Josiane Chriqui Feigon notes how the millennials' approach to work is radically different from the approach taken by the generations that preceded them: "The millennials are technically astute, have little patience for things they deem a waste of time and put a high value on work that they feel has meaning". Generation Y is keener to travel for either personal or professional reasons, more likely to challenge themselves and take risks, and more interested in experiences than rewards. The new generation is, make no mistake, global, and Generation Z, which is following fast on the heels of the millennials, will almost certainly be even more so. We no longer measure skill sets or proficiencies locally; they are now measured globally. Connectivity is ceaseless and ubiquitous; boundaries have evaporated as mobility has increased, and the digital natives have grown up to utterly master this new reality.

As the leader of a sales organisation, you must be aware not only that this change has happened but also what the consequences of this change are. Young candidates see their time as more of an investment, and, before they commit to anything, they will focus on the *why*. Whereas careers in the past were measured based on the size of the paycheque that you could bring home, today's most desirable candidates want to work for a company that is changing the world (even if in a relatively small way). They want to be shown, not the pot of gold at the end of the rainbow, but the company's vision for the future, and particularly the role they can play in helping the organisation realise that vision.

What this means for recruiting in sales-centric businesses

Times are rapidly changing and, as a leader, you must embrace change. When I started working in sales in the '90s, there was a general consensus surrounding what good skills and traits a successful salesperson should possess. Everyone may have come from different backgrounds, but decades of 'old-school' sales had created a general agreement surrounding effective sales practices. Cold calling remained as the sales tool of first and most frequent resort; email campaigns were on the rise, but were seen as substantially less effective than cold calling. Inside sales was just beginning to achieve scalability and higher performance, transitioning from un-glorified telemarketing to a mainstream sales channel.

Since the Digital Revolution changed buyers as much as it did sellers, it soon became apparent that the old models desperately needed to be modernised. Large organisations (particularly those that wanted to get or remain ahead of the curve) began investing billions into understanding future trends and leveraging social networks. Those who were savviest in the new technologies tended to be in their twenties, so organisations began, first to consider, and then to hire young, talented candidates, many of them lacking the credentials that were once standard. Education and professional experience were now only partial indicators. What mattered most was a combination of goal-setting abilities, curiosity and digital fluency.

The lesson to be learned from these organisations and their early movement into uncharted digital territory is that, when MNCs moved quickly and made it clear that they were more concerned with where the market was heading than where it was they became magnets for precisely the kind of talent that could help build a bridge to where they wanted to be. It did wonders for their brands among the millennials, and today's wisest sales leaders are the ones who are simultaneously working on their approach to candidate sourcing and creating a strong brand that shows customers and candidates that the organisation is forward-thinking and adaptable.

As candidates, millennials will come to interviews having done their homework in ways that might surprise you. If you have made your organisation an attractive one for GenY candidates, they will come to interviews armed with a wealth of information about your organisation, your customer network, and perhaps even you. Even the interviews themselves will defy expectations. Recently, between the first and second round of interviews with a candidate, I found myself doubting his professionalism. He had not even brought anything to take notes on. When I brought him in for a second interview, though, with incredible attention to detail, he immediately picked up right where we had left off. When I told him about my initial misgivings later in the interview, he merely held up his smartphone—he had been taking notes on his phone during our conversations and even taking pictures while we were white-boarding. Technology has changed the game; the onus is on sales leaders to change with the times.

The millennial-friendly workplace

Becoming an attractive workplace for today's most desirable candidates means adopting some of GenY's relatively new approaches to information exchange. Don't be afraid to use videoconferencing technology to filter candidates, exchange information through instant messaging platforms, or use technology in the ways that digital natives do.

At the same time, don't throw the baby out with the bathwater when you target younger hires. There are many sales techniques that have stood the test of time for a reason, and you'll know which of those techniques candidates will need to master if they are to succeed in your industry. Be open to new ideas, but don't assume that every new idea is necessarily better than the one it will supposedly replace. Some basic traits will always differentiate great salespeople from mediocre ones. Later in this book we'll discuss these key traits in more detail.

Just remember that as a leader it is you who will be challenged the most. It's you who will be asked to evolve in your thinking and to raise the bar for those around you and for the organisation. Being able to distinguish an industry-changing innovation from a flash-in-the-pan fad will be important; you'll need to keep yourself agile enough to first understand and then to pivot quickly to embrace new trends.

Generations X and Y

There are plenty of new ways in which individuals proficient in using Web 2.0 can provide valuable insight into prospecting, qualifying and closing. Since GenY grew up in parallel with digital technology, they tend to master technology faster and more completely than most Gen Xers.

That said, sales performance doesn't come exclusively through mastering technology, and GenX can often spot what GenY misses, leveraging their experience and leadership traits to achieve success and even coaching the newer generations in the sure-fire sales techniques that complement their digital literacy.

Recent research has suggested that this wedding of GenY insight with GenX experience can be highly productive. According to a 2013 EY study, Gen Y can be relied upon to leverage the latest technologies in powerful and productive ways and to bring unflagging enthusiasm and optimism wherever they go. GenX are most effective in terms of management (better than both their GenY and boomer counterparts) and, again according to EY, they score highest when it comes to revenue generation, adaptability, problem-solving and collaboration.

By 2020, over 50 per cent of the global workforce will be made up of millennials. This means that tomorrow's top-performing organisations will be the ones that are able to build the strongest and longest-lasting bridges between their GenX and GenY employees. Here are a few tips that will help you ensure that inter-generational collaboration and cooperation are commonplace in your organisation:

- Team leaders and members alike should recognise that each generation has its distinctive strengths and weaknesses. Open communication between and among leadership and team members is crucial here. At every level, the ability to receive advice and feedback should be encouraged. In a heterogeneous sales team, the importance of this ability cannot be overstated.

- GenY people have been raised by their families to believe that their opinions are valuable. Once on the job, millennials will not let a lack of experience or subject matter expertise keep them from contributing. They expect to be heard out. Their perspective may not always give them insight, but dismissing them out of hand can lead to friction. Leverage their passionate desire to contribute to create a culture of cross-generational collaboration.

- Both GenX and GenY assign a great deal of importance to workplace flexibility and a concordant work/life balance. Your company should therefore consider providing flexible hours and measuring both generations based on outcomes rather than compliance to working hours and standard operating procedures.

- Millennials love to learn and develop new skills and competencies. Gen X enjoys management, coaching and mentoring. The mentoring possibilities this combination presents should not be ignored. As long as arrangements are open and flexible, there is potential to build an extremely effective coaching culture in which skill cross-pollination becomes a driver for employee development and lasting loyalty.

- Millennials see the workplace as a space in which personal goals and aspirations are enabled. The leadership team needs to leverage this powerful motivator to drive millennials' performance. This is where Angle Recruiting will prove itself as a powerful methodology.

CHAPTER 2:
WHERE CULTURES
COLLIDE

In the last chapter, I mentioned that millennials are open to travel (whether for professional or personal reasons, the drive to move beyond the parochial remains the same). Digital technology has undoubtedly made the world a smaller and more connected place, but there is more—much more—to it than that. Professionals, especially young and unattached ones, are more likely than ever to move beyond the cities and even countries in which they were raised and educated. Immigration and emigration are working hand in hand to create a richly diverse workplace in which cultures are colliding and blending at an unheard of rate.

This presents some unique challenges, but it presents just as many (if not more) opportunities. I want to help sales managers avoid some of the more common mistakes they make when attempting to manage an office in which cultures collide.

Before going any further, I want to tell you a little bit about myself, which might help explain why I am so passionate about the cross-cultural dimension of the modern workplace. I am, by birth, Italian and, thanks to something of a sheltered upbringing, I grew up until the age of 14 without really knowing what a non-Italian was. I studied English and French, but the people who spoke these languages were always at arm's length. Everything that I knew about the foreign world was filtered by someone or something: the media, my school books, the translated texts I read, all sought to translate the outside world in easily digestible ways, assuring me that I could understand other cultures without ever directly experiencing them.

As a teenager, all of that changed. My first exposure to foreign nationals was at a resort (where I met my first girlfriend—a Belgian who helped me practise my French). The following summer, I made friends with a few kids from Eastern Europe, and their languages piqued my curiosity, so I started to learn Czech and Polish. Later, I worked as a swimming instructor, and one of my colleagues was Persian.

He regaled me with stories about the culture and the lifestyle in Iran. None of this experience fit with what I had been told about non-Italians as a young child.

As a young adult, I was presented with a choice: either I stay in Italy and build myself a life there or I explore what the world had to offer. I chose the latter. I have lived in six countries spanning three continents. I have travelled all over the world, and it was this travel that introduced me to a beautiful Indonesian woman who would later become my wife. After spending time in Spain and Egypt, I started looking for a big European capital where I could move to in order to develop my sales career. After an epic summer in France and England, I decided my next destination would have to be London. To achieve my career goals, I needed to study and work while I also looked for the right British university. It was at an open event at the London Metropolitan University where I met Fenty, a beautiful post-grad student and, within a few months of this fateful meeting, my wife as well. Travelling opens doors everywhere, and it still amazes me that one of those doors led me to a woman like Fenty and the incredible, global life we have shared together.

In my career, I have met scores of people like myself—those who have untethered themselves from the comforts of home and country to explore what the wide world has to offer. These are not itinerant wanderers (far from it).

They are professionals who boast a broad range of experiences and skills gleaned from the many cultures they have called home for a time. Like the millennials—indeed, they often *are* millennials—these culturally experienced professionals are looking for something beyond the superficial, something that is profoundly fulfilling. They are not keen to settle for anything less, so you'll want to create an environment in which these individuals can draw upon their wide-reaching experience and strengthen the organisation. Let's take a closer look at some of the strategies we can use to do just that.

The cross-cultural mindset: expanding frames of reference

As a sales manager, you almost certainly know the value of a quick set of reflexes. Not only do we want those we manage to respond quickly to the unexpected or the unusual, we also want them to respond in appropriate ways – that reflect an organisation-wide commitment to sensitivity and acceptance.

Learning how to react in this way comes from an expanded frame of reference. Every time we encounter something that is new to us, we leverage our personal frame of reference, which tells us, first, how to interpret it and, second, how to react to it. This frame of reference is shaped by our experiences, our beliefs and our values. Exposure to other cultures gives us the chance to see that each of these is not universal – not only do people entering a culture from outside often have different belief systems, they may also experience the world and assign value in very different ways. They might have different ways of evaluating success and failure; they might seek different modes of fulfilment and entirely different relationship structures.

As a leader, it's important to be aware of this (especially during the recruiting process). While it's not remotely helpful to discard all of your evaluation criteria, it is wise to expand your frame of reference before evaluating today's candidates. Everyone's frame of reference is at least partially inherited, and everybody's frame of reference is being adjusted—even if only minutely—as they process new experiences. The key to recruiting in the increasingly cross-cultural world is to allow the borders of your frame of reference to be supple; let them expand and evolve.

As leaders, it is our personal responsibility to make sure that nothing that is helpful is excluded. We must therefore be aware, not only of our own frame of reference, but also that those around us might also be prone to snap judgments. This can lead to misgivings and misunderstandings, and it's important to prepare for these. When cultures collide, some friction is inevitable; the role of leadership is to open up channels of communication and conciliation that make these issues resolvable and, perhaps more importantly, into teachable moments.

Four rules for doing business in a cross-cultural environment

Knowing that we are faced with complex issues and that – since business waits for no man – we have a limited amount of time to address them, it is helpful to have a few guiding principles when it comes to managing today's cross-cultural workplace. Experience has taught me a great deal about how best to do this and, from this experience, I have distilled four rules for doing business in a cross-cultural workplace. These rules have helped me (and those I have shared them with) prevent major issues while at the same time helping managers to take advantage of the many opportunities presented by the intermeshing of cultures.

Rule #1: Know your own culture

The first step to managing the cross-cultural workplace demands a bit of mirror-gazing; if we are to understand how different frames of reference are interacting, we must first understand our own frame of reference and the role it is playing in our judgments. To put this another way, we must be aware of how we think and interpret.

As an Italian, I tend to be extremely talkative. When I relocated to the UK, I started working side by side with English, Dutch and German people, and it became immediately apparent that talking everything out wasn't always the solution of choice. I needed to broaden my frame of reference.

I could have hired Italians to work on the Italian market, but this would have been discarding the strengths particular to the Dutch, German and English members of my team. Learning not to place snap value judgments on the different ways that people from different cultures interact and work made it possible to learn from and use these cultural differences to make the organisation more broadly appealing to its customers.

Take language for example. It is, of course, important that you are able to communicate with your team and that your team members can communicate with each another, but even when we understand the words we are hearing, we are often missing a great deal. Outputs and inputs pass through a cultural filter that can often produce unintended meanings. When we interact with those who are outside of our cultural framework, our brains are simply unprepared for the often-subtle clues so crucial to nuanced meaning. It's crucial to understand that, just as our own languages are freighted with nuance and idiom, so too are other languages. Even when everybody is trying to speak the same language, there might be a great deal of trial and error, apologies, and learning that needs to take place before we can be clear as crystal with each other.

It's not just language-based understanding that we need to look out for; it's also cultural differences that can lead to misunderstandings. Let me give you an example of this. Andrea, another ex-pat Italian and a dear friend of mine, lives in England with his Indonesian wife, Putri. In the early days of their marriage, he had to learn to navigate a minefield of concealed cultural clues; it was only through mutual understanding and patience that they managed to make it through these first few years with their marriage intact. One day, my wife and I were invited to their house for lunch. Andrea started telling us about the previous night's party. He mentioned that both he and Putri had had so much food that they "snored like trains" all night. While the guests didn't so much as bat an eyelid, Putri was appalled. Her privacy framework (a product of her Indonesian upbringing) had been violated, and what was intended as a bit of self-deprecating humour was interpreted as a betrayal of trust. Andrea was quick to apologise, and Putri was just as quick to forgive, but the misunderstanding had resulted in no small amount of awkwardness around the table.

In a business context, these kind of simple misunderstandings can be disastrous. Understanding our own framework is an important first step to avoiding the kinds of impasses that result from cultural insensitivity, but this isn't all. We also need to understand, as much as possible, the cultural framework of those with whom we're doing business.

Rule #2:Don't make assumptions. Be aware of the cultural context in which you are doing business

Our cultural framework affects (often in dramatic ways) how we do business. It might change whether a client expects short-term or long-term results, whether aggressive or passive negotiating styles will be effective, whether questions regarding discounts are a matter of course or highly inappropriate, or whether meetings can take place over the phone or must be face to face. If we want to be successful in business (especially when that business has a global reach), we must be aware of and sensitive to the various cultural frameworks we will encounter.

In Asia, where West and East most frequently collide, radically different business approaches can (and often do) lead to offence taken and given unintentionally. The risks to corporate or personal brand damage are substantial; indeed, one's credibility in both the market and the community is constantly at risk.

If you are (like me) a westerner living and working in Asia, almost every day you will have meetings with people possessing values and sensitivities very different to your own. A honed sense of cultural awareness and sensitivity is something you simply cannot do without. Make assumptions about something as simple as what kind of food or alcohol to serve at a function and those assumptions might scuttle a promising opportunity. The same goes for any business that is attempting to win foreign customers or otherwise establish a presence abroad. Educate yourself about your new cultural surroundings; take nothing for granted.

Rule #3:Project an image of one who has an open mind and can go with the flow

As a leader, you set the tone for how those around you will approach cultural differences. While it is immensely important that you understand as much as possible of both your own cultural framework and the different frameworks of those around you, it is also important that you project this understanding outwards. This is something that requires no small degree of emotional intelligence and openness.

The image to project as a leader is one of open-mindedness – one that shows a willingness to go with the flow, adopting and adapting to the requirements of the different cultures around you. When there has been a disconnect or a crossed wire (and there are bound to be some), show true leadership by reading the situation and demonstrating an understanding of where the misstep occurred. If an apology is necessary, offer one, but do so in a dignified way. A good leader knows the difference between genuflecting (occasionally necessary) and kowtowing (almost never necessary).

Rule #4:Let honest curiosity drive your questions

If you find yourself in doubt about what to do or say in a culturally sensitive situation, ask questions. Let these questions be transparent attempts to gain clarity, but also show that you are honestly curious. Cultural nuances, while absorbed by those who grew up in the culture, take time to absorb (and even more time to fully understand). By showing you are eager to learn from your mistakes, you'll be much more likely to turn a *faux pas* into a bridge-building opportunity.

This is especially pertinent when recruiting. During the interviews, be absolutely transparent about the position's roles and responsibilities. When there is a cultural gap between you and the candidate, pay close attention to body language and tone of voice. Allow the candidate to ask plenty of questions, but understand that some cultures don't place a great deal of value on inquisitiveness. Again, let your curiosity guide you to a deeper understanding of the candidate, their cultural frame of reference and the particular strengths (and weaknesses) that this frame of reference brings with it.

PART 2

The Sales Manager as Recruiter in Chief

CHAPTER 3:
SALES MANAGERS IN THE NEW WORLD

Whether it is the ins and outs of the digital age, the millennials, and the different approach to hiring that comes with them, or the increasingly cross-cultural environment that is becoming commonplace in the modern workplace, sales managers have a lot on their plate. They have to navigate the changes that are taking place in the market (particularly the changes in the ways that customers interact with brands, salespeople and products), but they also have to address the changes to the workplace brought on by a new breed of experience-driven employees and a shrinking world that is bringing a broader range of cultures under a single roof than ever before.

To successfully guide your organisation through these constantly shifting waters, it is absolutely crucial to begin hiring the right candidates in the right way. This might seem fairly obvious – indeed, it seemed obvious to me when I was a sales manager. I thought, "There are successful people everywhere (including myself). All I need to do is hire people who seem to be doing things the same way that I (and successful people like me) would do them. Easy!" When I couldn't find carbon copies of myself or of the successful people I admired, it become apparent that my approach was deeply flawed. I quickly learned that a successful approach to recruiting is not as simple as it might seem.

Let's start by looking at some of the dos and don'ts that every sales manager should use as guidelines for powerful 21st-century recruiting practices.

Dos

Strike a delicate balance between slow and hasty decision-making

When I started managing a sales team within an IT consulting company, I inherited an existing team. Immediately, I thought that the team members were not exactly who I would have hired.

I saw a couple of people with good potential, but at least two thirds of the team was struggling – though all of them for different reasons.

I found that I was almost immediately under quite a bit of pressure to assess the quality of my AEs. Before I could get to know my team members, I had to start deciding who would make the cut and who wouldn't. Quick decision-making is a virtue among sales managers, but hasty decisions are only accidentally good ones. In the case of my experience with the IT consulting company, by responding to the pressure without first taking the time to consider the possible outcomes, I started off on the wrong foot with my team and it was a long time before I regained their trust.

Whether firing or hiring, it is equally important to consider each in good measure. In most organisations, the expectation will be that 90 per cent of new hires are successful. When we are hiring large numbers of new people, it is to be expected that some of the hires won't work out and that those who don't fit in will cause business disruptions. Because of that, we must make sure to, on one hand, listen to our gut feelings (positive and negative) and, on the other, to leverage our hiring practices with as much data as possible. Your hiring plan should prioritise all aspects of team management that can make a meaningful impact on sales performance, morale and ultimately, on the overall success of each member of your team.

Take the time during interviews and meetings to learn as much as you can about the candidate or employee

As a sales manager, you probably have a few bad hires and fires on your conscience. I know I do. When I look back at these, it is clear that what I should have done (and didn't do) with almost all of them was take the time to intimately understand who the individual was and what was (or was not) driving them. If I could have leveraged them the right way from the beginning, if I could have established the right expectations from the outset, things might have turned out differently. If you're not doing so already, here are a few best practices to help make your interactions with your employees more meaningful:

- Ask them to be specific about their goals and aspirations; the same goes for the challenges they have faced in both their business and their private life.
- Clarify boundaries. Your organisation's culture has definite boundaries and so do the people (you included) that work there. By discussing core values and expectations in terms of etiquette etc., you can save yourself a lot of time and energy down the road. When clarifying boundaries, ask for and provide clear and unambiguous answers.

- When establishing or clarifying boundaries and expectations, be aware of two important guidelines:
  - What you permit you promote.
  - Pick your battles; it's impossible to fight and win every conflict.
- Wind your watch: as we've discussed above, it's important to find the balance between over- and under-reaction. The best senior leaders are the ones who have this down to a fine art. When there are issues with team-member behaviour, learn to spot when the situation demands a hair-trigger reaction and when it demands a more measured response. This will help you defuse emotionally charged situations without damaging your (or the organisation's) reputation.
- Remember to learn as much as possible about your business partners as well. The more you know about how *they* measure success, the clearer you can be with your new or old team members about what is expected of them.

Keep your personal and business headaches outside of interviews

As I've emphasised above, today's most desirable candidates are seeking an experience more than they are seeking rewards.

Allow your personal or business headaches to bubble to the surface during interviews and it's unlikely that your organisation will appear in its best light. It'll be impossible to get the candidate excited about joining a team when there's any doubt surrounding whether or not you (or the organisation) will bear up under the strain for another quarter.

While honesty is important, so are first impressions. I've watched some fantastic candidates walk out the door, never to return, thanks to a less-than-ideal attitude or energy level on my part.

Don'ts

Don't assume that you understand the dynamics of the team you are assembling unless you've invested some time into doing so

The most successful managers always push themselves further by looking deeper. They aren't content with understanding their team and its dynamics superficially. They dig deep to find the best in their team, which makes it easier to motivate and inspire those they manage. It's quite common for managers (especially new ones) to focus the lion's share of their attention and energy on those the furthest ahead and the furthest behind the curve. With more experience, sales managers generally learn to step back and take a wider view. You'll want to avoid making assumptions about those that might be slipping under your radar. By working to grow your understanding of your team, you'll be able to recognise when a candidate is a perfect fit. Remember, the best managers don't just work to increase performance at the bottom and the top of the performance spectrum. They engage at every level.

Don't go looking for a 'mini me'

Most sales managers have at some time or another been guilty of this. They tend to look for the same qualities in candidates that they themselves possess. As understandable as it might be, try to avoid this tendency. While the unique skillset that you possess might be responsible for your success, there is already one you in the organisation. The skills or mindsets that might have worked for you won't necessarily work for others. This doesn't mean you need to go to the opposite extreme, but it does mean that you need to pay attention to the dynamics of the team and find somebody who is best suited for the position or role that needs to be filled. Being able to recognise this tendency in yourself will also give you the ability to spot interviewees who are better mimics than they are candidates.

Don't try to copy the style of senior sales managers

Speaking of mimics, you'll want to avoid copying the style of successful senior managers. Once again, this comes down to a nuanced understanding of team dynamics. Chances are, your senior colleagues have found success because they are operating in an environment that they know well. They've proved that they know how to blend disparate skillsets and mindsets together to build something powerful and lasting. If anything is worth copying, it is this – not department-specific management or recruiting practices.

Don't ignore what your gut is telling you (especially not when your gut reaction is a strongly negative one)

When I was young and bold – working in Egypt's leisure industry – I was asked to manage a team of six professional entertainers. The leader who preceded me had created a good blend of skillsets and mindsets, but it was immediately apparent that we needed to add two new members to the team. One of these new members was a young and extremely attractive woman and, though my gut told me that what I was doing was wrong, I began a romantic relationship with her almost immediately. The team dynamics changed palpably for the worse overnight. The relationship soon came to my manager's attention, and I was promptly asked to leave the organisation. Brief though it was, this – my first experience in management – taught me a lesson I'll never forget (and one that I frequently return to when recruiting): when your gut tells you to avoid something or someone, heed its advice.

Don't feel the need to always be in the right

When it comes to recruiting, not every decision you make will be the right one. I've mentioned above that even good hiring practices lead to an attrition rate for new hires of around 10 per cent. In my career, I've tried to hire nice people; some of these have turned out to be great AEs, others not so much. When I was still new to managing, I wanted to justify each and every one of my hiring decisions; I wanted to prove that I could spot the diamond in the rough before anybody else; I wanted to be acknowledged for the coaching work I had done with the AE (even when that coaching work had come to nothing); in short, I wanted to show that I had been right all along, even when I hadn't been. Great leaders don't always make the right decision, but they know how to react when the consequences of a poor decision come to call.

When I was still fairly new to sales management, I interviewed what I thought was a great candidate for a role in my growing team. He was highly educated, he carried himself with dignity, and it was clear that the man had integrity. I was happy to make him a part of my team, but after a few weeks I started receiving feedback from all departments telling me he wasn't going in the right direction. I was convinced that he was a slow burner and that he just needed time and would eventually prove everybody wrong (and me right). If I had looked at the situation with eyes unclouded, it would have been easy to see that my new hire just wasn't right for the company and for the territory that he had to manage. The fallout lasted for months. Revenue flattened out and client relationships soured. If I had been willing to claim the mistake as my own from the beginning, all of it could have been avoided.

CHAPTER 4:

THE FOUNDATION: PUNCTUALITY CONSISTENCY AND CLARITY

While we don't have to be perfect, we can expect three things from those around us (and from ourselves as well). These three qualities are the building blocks of successful leadership practice and they tend to inspire emulation. No matter what the individual's position or responsibilities, whether they are customer-facing or not, without these three qualities, performance will always be sub-par. In terms of expectations, they represent the bare minimum—we can accept nothing less from ourselves, and we can expect nothing less from our colleagues and team members.

We must be **Punctual**. When interviewing a candidate, both interviewer and interviewee must be punctual. For the former, it shows respect and makes a very clear statement about what the candidate can expect from the organisation; for the latter, it shows that he or she recognises that they recognise an opportunity when it is presented to them and it also sets the tone in terms of the kind of personal and professional conduct the organisation can expect.

We must be **Consistent.** Our word is our bond, and we want to make it clear from the outset that our words are meaningful, that we can be depended upon to follow through on our promises, and that a deep sense of integrity informs our actions and our decisions. Although it might be difficult to show or assess this quality during interviews, we can, at the very least, show that we and the organisation we represent are both utterly transparent.

We must be **Clear.** By being clear (and expecting and even demanding clarity from candidates), we can significantly lower the attrition rate. Managers and candidates both have expectations, but both can be reluctant to discuss these expectations openly during the interviews, turning these interviews into pitch sessions – which rarely provide either party with the clarity that they will need to manage and meet expectations. Be clear and seek clarity from the outset.

By being punctual, consistent and clear, and by expecting members of our team (new or old) to display these same qualities, we can attract and retain top industry talent and our niche's most desirable customers as well. These qualities may not be enough on their own (to say they are all one needs would be a gross oversimplification), but they are the foundation upon which all other successful business and hiring practices are built. Let's take a closer look at each of them.

Punctuality

On the way to Bali, I opened a newspaper to an advertisement, which read: "Trading trust and timeliness: take the time to manage your time. Being on time is a sign of respect for the people who buy our time. We transact promptness for trust, both of which are invaluable commodities we trade with one another". In business and in life, trust is a very important commodity that we trade with those we rely upon to help us achieve our personal goals. Punctuality is the first and most important way to build trust. It boils down to setting and meeting expectations and respecting commitment. Punctuality gives the true measure of how we value the time of people with whom we are working or doing business. It goes beyond etiquette and cultural habits. The moment we translate 'time' into 'respect', everything becomes clearer. We wouldn't disrespect our client on purpose, and we would never say outright to our employees that their time and commitment are of no value. If we respect clients and employees (and of course friends and family members), it follows that we should be habitually punctual – this is the only way to show that we respect others and their time.

Consistency

A good friend of mine (we'll call him 'Rob') recently left the American MNC he had been with for quite some time. The structures were, he said at the time, too rigid and, with an impressive resumé, he wanted to see what the job market had to offer. He quickly found a start-up with an innovative and highly promising software platform. The company had just started a big expansion and had received substantial funding from a group of international investors. They were looking for somebody with Rob's kind of experience, so this seemed like the opportunity he was looking for. Here was his chance to work hand-in-hand with senior management to build a business of which everybody could be proud.

During the interviews, everything looked like a perfect fit. From the reporting structure and company culture to the exact scope of his duties, the CEO painted a picture of the organisation and Rob's role in it that seemed to fit exactly what Rob was looking for. He was told that he would report directly to the CEO, that he would be MD for his region, and that he would be independent – empowered to mould a high-performing sales team already brimming with talent.

Everything looked perfect until Rob was introduced to a senior executive with the organisation. When Rob asked the executive the same questions that the CEO had answered during the interviews, the executive's honest and detailed answers painted a picture of the organisation very different from the one painted by the CEO. The reporting structure was not as transparent as he had been told it would be; the flat organisation that Rob had found so appealing was far more hierarchical than he had been led to believe – almost identical to the old MNC world that he had left behind.

Rob was determined to remain positive, and he took the position, only to leave the organisation a short time later when it became clear that the inconsistency he had encountered early on was in no way an isolated incident.

There's a lot of focus on positivity in today's business literature, and a positive attitude certainly goes a long way in sales organisations, but don't let your positivity turn into naiveté. We've already talked about listening to your gut, and the naive tend to be those who either ignore or can't hear their gut when it speaks to them. Rob was so enthusiastic about leaving the corporate world and working for a promising start-up that he says now that it must have been masochism that kept him from running for the hills the moment he encountered inconsistent messaging from management. Inconsistency is often the symptom of much larger issues beneath the surface.

Clarity

During my conversations with sales leaders and entrepreneurs, one of the recurring topics is the need for clarity in these less-than-clear times. This is especially pertinent when we are recruiting. Clarity from the outset about what people are expected to do once they start working for us invariably leads to team members who meet or even surpass expectations.

How often during interviews do we sidestep discussions related to aspects of the position that might turn out to be deal breakers? This mistake costs organisations thousands of dollars in wasted training, missed performance and damage to the brand.

Being crystal clear as to our expectations and our measure of success from the very beginning prepares candidates for what they will encounter when they join the team, and it allows them to make an informed decision. The more vague you are during the recruiting process, the more likely become uncomfortable conversations down the road. As a sales manager, when you are transparent in terms of expectations, you give yourself future leverage. Clarity also builds trust and creates a predictable environment in which our team can compete, succeed and even overachieve.

Align expectations during candidate interviews by following these three steps:

1. Before the recruitment process starts, write down:
    a. what the worst day and the best day at work will look like
    b. a precise description of how team members are measured (including what you will need to see if you are to endorse their career progression)
    c. a description of the expected challenges associated with the position (this should be balanced with descriptions of the support that will be provided).
2. During the interview, go over everything that you wrote down during step one with the candidate, giving them plenty of time to ask clarifying questions.

3. Once you are sure that there is clarity between you and the candidate, ask them to provide feedback and to confirm that, knowing what they now know, there is still interest in the position.

Before I implemented this three-step process, I struggled to find the right time to set expectations. As soon as I started preparing, discussing and clarifying during every interview, I found greatly improved levels of trust between me and the candidate (which frequently translated to higher levels of trust between manager and employee later on). I also found that increased clarity about roles and expectations led to higher levels of activity and performance from new hires.

PART 3

Angle Recruiting

CHAPTER 5:
ANGLE RECRUITING OVERVIEW

During my days as an engineer and, later on, when I got into the advisory business, I got used to drawing up detailed and precise project timelines, which demanded that I understand (as completely as possible) the organisation's past (as it was), its present (as it is) and its future (as it will be) status. In the hundreds of interviews I have conducted, I would use timelines that would help candidates visually explain their career plans and ambitions. It was only a matter of time before I connected these two practices and recognised the unmistakable similarity between organisational and candidate timelines.

Like organisational timelines, which illustrate a company's entrepreneurial journey, candidate timelines trace a similar line – a journey that may have many parallels. Organisations, like people, have a past, present and future; they have short-term targets (milestones) and long-term targets (vision). It is possible to trace, for individuals and organisations alike, a line through space and time that clearly reflects where they have been, where they are, and where they'd like to go in the future.

Lay the ideal candidate's timeline over that of the organisation and, though the candidate's line will be shorter than that of the organisation, there should be no difference between the two in terms of trajectory. The two should overlap at each significant milestone. Compare an inappropriate candidate's timeline with that of the organisation and the two lines will diverge sharply (perhaps never meeting at all). Since the in-all-ways-perfect candidate is largely chimerical, almost all candidates should have a small or large angle that separates the two trajectories.

Angle Recruiting is about discovering this angle and using it as a powerful tool to help you assess a candidate's fitness for a particular position within your organisation. It is a proven recruitment methodology that takes the guesswork out of deciding whether or not to hire a candidate for a specific position within your organisation. It allows sales managers to attract, select and retain the right candidates and to put them in the right positions.

The Angle Recruiting methodology covers the following four stages of recruiting:

1. identifying your organisation's needs and writing a powerful job description
2. sourcing the right candidates(if we want to put the right people into our recruitment funnel, we first need to identify the right recruitment channels)
3. interviewing the candidates in ways that allow us to angle correctly, selecting the right candidates for the right role and for the right reasons
4. selecting that is rigorous and onboarding that is fast and effective.

I developed this methodology over years spent recruiting and interviewing candidates from diverse backgrounds in completely different geographies. I saw the frustrations, the lost productivity, and the toxic work environment that were the result of outdated recruiting practices.

My first mentor told me that, just as water constantly seeks a channel to the sea, people can be counted on to follow their own dreams. Too many sales managers forget this when they're recruiting. As we'll see, identifying the organisation's needs is only the first step of the interviewing stage. Angle Recruiting's most important feature is its ability to strike a balance between the needs of the organisation and those of the individual who is being recruited. During the interviewing stage of Angle Recruiting, you'll be able to do five things that will help you strike that all-important balance. You'll learn how to:

- **define** your organisation's DNA and its needs
- identify the **you now** for the candidate
- identify the **you tomorrow** for candidate
- support the candidate as they build a **plan** that will help them achieve their goals
- assure that there is a **match** between the organisation and the candidate and that the relationship will be symbiotic, with each helping the other to achieve their goals.

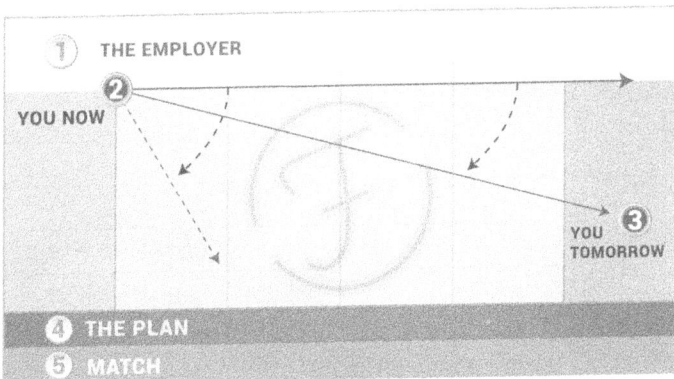

Angle Recruiting makes the hiring process more scientific. From the first, the aim of the method has been to produce tangible (and repeatable) results and this is exactly what it has done. Organisations that have allowed Angle Recruiting to guide their hiring practices have witnessed measurable improvements in workplace morale and performance and reduced churn. To put it simply, the method works. Let's begin.

CHAPTER 6:
THE JOB DESCRIPTION

Not every organisation prepares a job description (JD) at the beginning of the recruiting process. Very small organisations often skip this important step, opting to do their hiring in channels that don't require them. However, even if the channels you'll be recruiting in don't require a JD, preparing one will help you a great deal when it comes to the interviewing stage of Angle Recruiting. Writing a JD will give you the clarity surrounding your organisation's needs and the role's requirements that will help you zero in on the candidate that will not only meet requirements but satisfy deeper needs as well.

For most sales managers, JDs are a matter of course. Even in medium-sized organisations, they're an essential feature of the recruiting process. Due to immutable principles of impermanence, your business will always be changing, which means that the roles and responsibilities of your team members will also be in flux. The need to bring new people on board might be due to any number of factors: perhaps you are scaling up your sales capacity; you might be replacing people who moved on (or were removed) from the organisation; or you could be changing the sale structure, and it looks like it will be less expensive to add new people with the necessary skills than it will be to retrain existing sales staff.

Whatever the reason, you've determined that you need to add new staff. You'll have to do some careful thinking about exactly *why* you're adding to your headcount. New employees mean a sizable investment of time, energy and money – not to mention the complexity involved in managing a larger team. I'm constantly amazed at how many companies decide to add new employees without first thinking long and hard about whether a new member of the team is really necessary – there might be alternatives to hiring that you haven't considered.

Getting started: a few important things to consider

I'm going to assume that you have put considerable thought into this and that you are quite sure recruiting is the answer to your organisation's issues. Here's what you need to know before you start preparing a JD:

- What are your organisation's goals for the next 12-24 months?
- What are the unique features of your corporate culture that will make your organisation more or less attractive to candidates? If, for example, you have a fresh and agile corporate culture with a flat organisation, you must be aware of it. Not all organisations grow in the same way. Some companies end up being very hierarchical with very strong governance, others have more flexible reporting structures and few leaders (flat). Different structures create different expectations in the minds of candidates. Candidates who are not used to certain company structures may find them difficult to cope with. At the same time, other candidates may actively seek out these company setups.
- What will the candidate have to achieve in order to be deemed successful? How will this success contribute to corporate strategy?
- What metrics will be used to measure the candidate's success?

- What are the specific skills successful candidates will need to possess? Are there any industry- or role-specific certifications, linguistic skills or IT skills that will be required?

- What kinds of traits (professional or personal) should the ideal candidate for the position possess? We'll explore this at greater length later on, but it's important to think about this before you even write the JD. Just as with skills, there might be specific traits, without which even otherwise-well-qualified candidates will struggle to find success.

- What kind of experience will you expect candidates to have? As experienced practitioners of performance-based recruitment will tell you, a candidate's track record speaks volumes about what the candidate is capable of. Mind that in many industries, we are seeing a trend of hiring very young individuals who gain valuable experience as they ascend through the ranks. If this is a route you're considering, experience will be less relevant, but you might want to give a little more weight to academic performance. I want to stress here that some of my greatest recruiting successes have been with candidates who had neither the experience nor the academic performance to make them seem like an instant match. Angle Recruiting is particularly good at identifying candidates who might not jump out at you on paper but will, nevertheless, be an excellent fit for your organisation.

All of these guidelines will help you gain clarity surrounding the kind of candidate you are looking for, and the more clarity you have the easier it will be for business partners involved in the recruitment process to narrow down the search.

A few words on experience: One of my mentors in Singapore once told me to watch out for people claiming to have over ten years of experience as they may actually have one year of experience repeated ten times. At the same time, candidates who have successfully filled a number of different sales roles during their careers are far more valuable than candidates with longer tenures in a single role. Say Candidate A has been selling computers to British organisations for 10 years. Candidate B has only been selling for six years, but two of these years were spent selling to British organisations, two years to French organisations, and two years to Japanese organisations. Though Candidate A has four years on Candidate B in terms of sales experience, the breadth of Candidate B's experience could potentially make them a much stronger candidate.

Do some thinking about what you want 'relevant experience' to mean. Relevance is a matter of perspective;

its meaning changes from person to person, market to market, and role to role. When you're starting to prepare your JD, be precise when it comes to describing what kind of relevant experience your ideal candidate will possess.

When you're preparing to write a JD, try to interact with your business partners as much as possible. Put yourself in multiple shoes: your new hire will have to interact with several people, each of them with his or her own requirements. Make sure to identify the individual whose role will be most affected by the new hire and involve them in the planning and composition of the JD. Doing so will save you headaches later on (especially during the onboarding stage).

Composing your JD

Once you've got the prep work out of the way, you are ready to start composing the JD. For best results, there are a few best practices that you'll want to follow:

Think about the channel

We'll talk about this more in the next chapter, but the point bears repeating: today's digital job market means that you're almost certain to target social networks (LinkedIn, Facebook, et al.) and other web portals. Make sure you keep these channels in mind so that you won't have to rewrite the JD every time you change channels. Remember, your JD will come across very differently in different channels. It's always wise to make the JD easy to read (avoid unnecessary jargon). Highlight must-read sections and provide a more complete, downloadable JD in case potential candidates want to know more about the position.

JD components: introduction

It's wise to include a summary at the beginning of the JD. This should highlight the company's high-level and long-term vision and mission. Reference existing team members, focusing on what it is about their experience with the company and the management team that makes the organisation such an attractive workplace. Keep the language informal and colloquial. The introduction should set the tone for the rest of the JD; it should also reflect the corporate culture – if the language is stiff or overly formal, potential candidates might assume the same of the organisation itself. That might be the message you want to send, but, if it's not, try to address the reader in the same kind of language you would use in an informal meeting. Be sure to mention precisely what the role is meant to achieve and how this achievement will contribute to the overall strategy.

If you create an introduction that is detailed and engaging enough, it should be able to stand on its own on social media. The main purpose is to create interest, to, in effect, 'sell' the role and the organisation to potential candidates. Collaborate with Marketing to produce the desired effect (chances are, they'll know exactly how to target the kind of candidates you're after).

JD components: body

In the body of your JD, you'll want to highlight two things: expectations and requirements. Start with the former. Be precise about what will be expected of a new employee and how success will be measured. Touch on both measurable metrics and intangibles (e.g. attitude and behaviour). Touch on the challenges that the candidate will face, but don't linger on them (provide enough detail to be clear, but not so much that you labour the point). The section on expectations should also include a description of the team that the candidate will be joining.

The section on requirements should highlight the skills that will be required. Be precise in terms of what kind of documentation will be required. Is a CV enough, or will you require a more meticulously documented track record? I talked above about how setting arbitrary minimums (10 years of experience or more, for instance) can be problematic. I suggest a focus on achievements. Even a relatively short track record of excellence is better than a long but spotted work history. If there are specific and valuable skills, mindsets, or habits that you are particularly interested in, include this information as well.

Conclude the body of the JD with a clear call to action. Make it clear what channels are preferred for applications. If the candidate feels that they, and the position as you have described it, are a good match, the conclusion should compel them to begin working on their application immediately.

Promoting the JD

Once the JD is ready, make sure you share it with all relevant stakeholders. Many companies leverage multiple channels when they post their JDs. You might consider including a video or other unconventional media. A video can be a great way to highlight your organisation's culture to high-level candidates. YouTube videos are becoming almost commonplace for advertising or marketing roles, and it's only a matter of time before other industries catch up. The amount of work that top-level branding organisations are doing in this field is making it increasingly clear that promoting a JD with a video is something almost everybody will be doing soon.

When it comes to preparing and promoting the JD, the stakes couldn't be higher. Since it directly affects the pool of candidates from which you'll make your selection, procrastinating for too long or delegating to the wrong people will only produce the hoped-for results accidentally. Even if the position you're advertising is perfectly suited to the ideal candidate you're looking for, the JD needs to be persuasive enough that they are compelled to submit an application. Designing an effective JD is something that can make your recruitment process more powerful and more effective. It's the first step to setting your growing team up for a more successful future.

CHAPTER 7:
SOURCING

As a sales leader, you need to make sure you are regularly interviewing candidates. Especially in high-performing sales teams, there is a perpetual need for new team members. As your team grows, you will need more account managers. As business development reps become more effective in their target markets, the demand for new team members will rise (sometimes steadily and sometimes sharply).

If you have the opportunity to work for a fast-growing organisation, you'll be faced with a challenge familiar to sales managers in successful companies the world over: how to locate and address the great candidates that can add capacity and skills to your team. When it comes to sourcing, there are dozens of alternative. You'll need to consider a number of factors (budget, strategy, needs, region- or market-specific requirements, etc.) before deciding which avenue to explore. In general, smaller organisations will need to outsource candidate sourcing and possibly a portion of the recruitment function as well. Larger organisations and their economies of scale allow for an internal recruitment team. We'll explore each of these in turn below.

If your organisation is experiencing a dip in profits or new business, you might be approaching recruiting from an entirely different angle – seeking to replace low-performing employees with high-performing ones for instance. The fact is that, sometimes, upskilling and coaching are not always enough to turn around struggling performance. If you want to replace under-performers with over-achievers without causing business disruptions, it is best to keep a deep bench of potential candidates who are ready to step forward and assume a role with the organisation on short notice.

To make your task easier, I have prepared the following list, which summarises the alternatives available to those who are preparing to drop a line in today's deep talent pool.

Sourcing candidates for organisations with an internal recruitment function

There are a number of different options when looking for candidates. The best strategy is to drop your line in a few channels (being sure to approach candidates in channel-appropriate ways). Let's look at a few of the sourcing options.

Recruiting via social media (LinkedIn, Facebook, G+, et al.)

Since the advent of the nexus of social, mobile, cloud and information, social media networks have only increased their already impressive reach and appeal. Take LinkedIn for instance: its talent management solutions have revolutionised the way recruiters look for candidates. Highly customisable research engines that comb through massive global databases of professionals are making it easier than ever for recruiters to find the proverbial needle in the haystack.

Depending on what kind of candidate you are looking for (particularly if you're looking for creative millennials), you might want to explore promoting the position on sites like Facebook and Twitter. If it's experienced professionals you're looking for, though, LinkedIn remains the recruiting site of first resort for most digitally savvy recruiters. As with all forms of online recruiting, you'll want to carefully tailor your searches, and if you post your JD online, prepare for a potentially preposterously large number of unqualified submissions. Remember as well that, in little or big ways, we all craft and mould our online personas in ways that cast us in our best light. Candidates who look too good to be true online or on paper might not be all they appear to be.

Employer branding

Recently, there has been an increased focus on using employer branding to attract more and higher-calibre talent. Companies like Universum and Glassdoor have expanded into dozens of new global markets. These companies—and the growing number of others like them—are operating in the area between HR and marketing. They are able to deliver talent research tailored to an organisation's needs; however, the quality of the output largely depends on the quality of the input. They have a great deal of data to work with, but you need to be extremely precise when it comes to defining your hiring requirements.

Career fairs

You can hire a booth or give a presentation at a career fair. These events are chock-a-block with job seekers. Those looking for work aren't necessarily the best candidates, though. The most desirable candidates are often those who are employed but keeping their options open. You're not likely to find these at job fairs, but that doesn't mean that recruiting at job fairs should be dismissed out of hand. Job fairs also mean a substantial investment of time without any guarantee of a desirable outcome. I suggest that you use them periodically if your candidate pipeline is empty or nearly so.

Career sites

You will find the same (or at least similar) challenges on career sites that you will find at career fairs. When you're starting to plan your JD or explore your sourcing options, career sites can provide necessary clarity in terms of what other organisations are publishing or what level of candidates are available in the broad job market. However, chances are you'll have to explore other options to find your ideal candidate. With the substantial pressure that professional social media sites are placing on career sites, there are doubts about their21st-century staying power.

Billboards

Billboards, if intelligently placed, can broadcast your recruiting message in ways that are difficult to ignore. What's more, forward-thinking companies are finding very creative ways to use billboard advertising to their advantage. A few years ago, Google proved how effective a billboard job posting could be with an anonymous billboard featuring a complex maths equation. The answer to the equation led candidates to a website featuring the job posting. As one of the world's most in-demand hirers, it was only a matter of time before word spread that the problem was a portal to the highly desirable position. The problem proved too difficult for many would-be applicants, though, which meant that the pool of applicants was manageable.

Referral programs

In my experience, referral programs have been highly successful. Whether internal or external, referrals are almost always based on in-depth knowledge of exactly what the organisation needs and what the stakes are in terms of brand. Due to the lack of investment of time and money, referrals can look like an ideal solution to recruiting issues, but they present some unique challenges:

- Candidates may have been prepared for the interview beyond what should be allowed, giving them an unfair leg up on their competition.
- There may be personal dynamics at play between the referee and the referred. Especially when the referral is internal, personal history can rear its head in unexpected ways that can do damage to the team and its chemistry.

As with all of the other sourcing options listed here, approach referrals with a degree of caution.

Alumni networks

Like referral programs, it is wise to approach candidates recommended by alumni networks carefully. The ever-growing social network has made it easier than ever to remain connected with former employees, many of whom were exemplary contributors who possessed (and may still possess) a profound understanding of the organisation's needs. These alumni may be able to identify high-quality candidates from their network, and these candidates should be duly considered. We should not, however, take it for granted that former employees are aware of the organisation's current needs. Make sure the candidate is subject to the same degree of scrutiny as any other before they are moved to the next stage in the recruitment process.

College recruitment (campus recruitment events)

We talked above about the millennials and their appeal to today's modern sales organisations. For companies that are looking to invest in younger, less-experienced candidates, colleges can be a gold mine. The risks of hiring inexperienced new staff are fairly obvious, so I won't go into them here, but I will suggest a few things that you can do to help alleviate these risks. If you're hiring from the shallow end of the experience pool, make sure you have a rock solid training program in place (this should include even basic sales capabilities and, of course, extensive product training). You might also want to institute a mentoring program that pairs new hires with senior team members.

Scholarships or sales academies

Large organisations may be able to partner with universities to provide internships. Graduates are attracted to the academic credits and the corporate experience and, if they are budding salespeople, the top-quality sales training is also a huge draw card. Sales academies can prove tremendously effective in terms of training in-house staff while, at the same time, attracting external candidates. Through these academies we can improve our workforce while also qualifying and coaching a limited number of bright young salespeople, who, by the end of the academy, might be ready to join the sales team. The real luxury of this approach is the time it gives the organisation to evaluate potential employees (it also gives them a chance to further evaluate their existing people). Since they require economies of scale, scholarships and sales academies are more of an option for larger organisations than they are for small ones. Most SMEs just don't have the necessary budget.

Open houses

Open houses give an organisation the chance to sell its working style and corporate culture. By targeting a narrow field of potential candidates, an open house can be a brand showcase for your company while at the same time it can give you a chance to see how candidates perform in both professional and social settings. Make sure to observe carefully to make the most out of open houses.

Cold calling

This is possible when organisations have a structured HR and recruitment department with sourcers, recruitment managers, coordinators and an IT infrastructure supporting this.

Usually organisations at this level of maturity need a human capital management system to keep track of all interactions and notes. Headhunters and recruitment agencies have found that, even in the digital age, cold calling remains a powerful recruiting technique. Social media, while undeniably the most commonly used channel, lacks the personal touch that comes with one-on-one interaction. Think of recruitment as a sales process: talent is the need, jobs the product, talented candidates the prospects. The most desirable candidates, like the most desirable customers, need to be the focus of the right mixture of engagement and persuasion. Taking this approach can substantially improve your organisation's recruiting capabilities.

Sourcing candidates for organisations without an internal recruiting function

If you don't have in-house recruitment personnel or the resources you need to scour the market for the ideal candidate, this doesn't mean you have to settle for sub-par candidates. There are a number options available to organisations without an internal recruiting function. Let's take a closer look at some of them.

Recruitment agencies

Recruitment agencies usually have a large portfolio of qualified candidates. Depending on the size of the agency and how long it's been around, they should be able to do a good job of matching your organisation's needs with an available candidate. The issue is that most recruitment agencies are sales-driven organisations, meaning they have their own bottom line in mind when it comes to placing a candidate. Before working with a recruitment agency, double check that their due diligence and internal code of conduct are clear and fully transparent. The world of recruitment is unfortunately full of agencies that will prep and even coach candidates before interviews; this can (and does) lead to hires that are made under what are essentially false pretences. In the long term, this is a losing business strategy for the agency (it's just a matter of time before word spreads about the agency's lack of integrity and transparency). In the short term, though, the practice can be quite profitable.

Recruitment advisers and outsourcers

The lack of resources, together with cowboy recruitment agencies, have given an opportunity to HR professionals leaving the corporate world to set up their own practice and create freelance or outsource options that give SMEs access to recruiting skills previously unattainable – and often at a reasonable price to boot. The outsourced recruiter is charged with achieving a business result and charges a fee for the service delivered. It can be a great way for smaller organisation to scale up their business without dropping much-needed focus from business-critical priorities. If you are a small or medium-size business, you may, depending on where your business is located, be eligible for government subsidies for these services, so this is definitely a recruiting method to explore. If you choose to go with a recruitment adviser or outsourcer, seek clarity about the provider's business model, especially when it comes to how they collaborate with recruitment agencies.

Headhunters

Headhunters often boast a highly specialised set of skills and a deep network of industry contacts. They will give you access to a pool of highly skilled professionals, many of whom are not actively seeking employment – though they are keeping their options open. These skills and connections usually combine for excellent results, but these results, as you might expect, come with a premium price tag attached. For those who use headhunters, the investment has often proved worthwhile.

Professional organisations

Your local chamber of commerce, foreign associations or government association may have access to a large database of individuals with the kind of experience and skillsets you're looking to add to your team. Research the association to see if it might be a possible source of talent. If it is, consider a mutually beneficial partnership with the association.

A word on leveraging big data and analytics for recruiting

The digital age has brought with it a host of new technology-enabled ways to source candidates. I've highlighted the ways that social media (especially professional networks) can be a rich source of candidate insight, but the last few years have seen an explosion in the use of big data and analytics. Increasingly sophisticated information management technologies combined with the cloud and social media are allowing tech-savvy organisations to leverage big data and analytics during their recruitment processes. The number of big data companies is growing every year, and the recruiting potential of the technology is almost limitless. Providers like Butch Works, Riviera Partners and others are opening the way to the future, allowing organisations access to a wealth of information about candidates that enables them to predict relatively accurately the likelihood that they will (or will not) be successful in a particular role. This may significantly change the way that recruiting works in the future, but for now, it is nicely complementing recruiting practices in large organisations. There might only be a handful of companies out there truly taking advantage of everything big data and analytics have to offer, but the potential is so great that this is almost certain to become a cornerstone of future recruiting practices. If you want to stay ahead of the curve in terms of recruiting (and if you're reading this book, you almost certainly do), keep a close eye on this technology and its applications.

CHAPTER 8:

INTERVIEWING (THE PRE-INTERVIEW)

STEP 1: DEFINE THE ORGANISATION AND ITS NEEDS

We've come now to the heart of the Angle Recruiting Method. This is the part of recruiting that is most difficult to get right, and so, in the next three chapters we'll take a close look at the interviewing strategies that can help you assess candidates more effectively while, at the same time, making your organisation much more attractive to candidates (remember, you need to sell the organisation just as much as the candidate needs to sell him or herself).

I've mentioned a few times now that there are five steps in the interviewing process: 1) define your organisation and its needs; 2) you now; 3) you tomorrow; 4) planning; 5) matching. The first step is part of the pre-interview process, the second and third steps are part of the first interview, and the fourth and fifth steps are part of the second interview. Each of these steps will have its own chapter, so we'll look closely at each in turn, starting with the important step of defining your organisation and its needs.

Define your organisation and its needs

Ideally, this will be twice-covered ground. When you were preparing your JD, you should have taken a long, hard look at your organisation and its needs. As you prepare for the interview, you'll want to go over for a second time what you uncovered then. Depending on your company's approach to organisational self-awareness, this may be a step you can jog through. One of my former employers empowered recruiting practices by making sure that, no matter what department they were in, employees were expected to be able to sell the organisation as an employer. There were substantial rewards for employees that referred successful candidates, so everybody did their homework, boning up on the company's mission and vision and practising pitching the organisation to potential candidates.

Large organisations that depend on aggressive recruiting strategies have learned to leverage their employees in this way, and SMEs are learning to do the same thing. It turns your employees into a massive (and highly motivated) recruiting resource.

One of my early mentors taught me the five P rule: Poor Preparation Prepares for Poor Performance (he actually taught me a more-explicit seven P rule, but I'll keep it clean here). This nugget of alliterative wisdom applies to just about everything, and especially to interviewing. We need to be able to summarise where the company has come from, what its current status is, and where it sees itself five years from now. You'll probably want to define as precisely as possible the key milestones that the organisation will have to cross if it is to remain on the right path.

All this preparatory work should be done with four things in mind:

1. We need to be honest with candidates: The interview stages are our chance to build trust with candidates. To make sure this trust is a lasting one, we need to make sure that the definition we prepare reflects reality – not fantasy.

2. We need to be positive and inspiring: Every company faces its challenges, and we want to be clear about these from the outset, but, in order to remain positive and inspiring, we need to balance challenges with opportunities.

3. We need to be prepared to discuss vision, not details: Preparing for interviews by piling up a mountain of financial data or detailed descriptions of the business model is almost always wasted time. Since it's easier to sell a vision (how the organisation is changing the world or the lives of its clients) your preparation should focus on these aspects more than on the financial particulars.

4. We need to be passionate: Candidates want to see the organisation's culture reflected in the person who is interviewing them, so get ready for the interview by preparing a high-level personal-value description that details precisely how the organisation has contributed directly to your personal and professional success. This process can be aided by Simon Sinek's Golden Circle methodology, which starts with the most important question of all: Why is your company in business? Companies with a clear reason to be in business (something that goes well beyond making profits for their investors) are able to attract and inspire employees and clients. Such companies attract and retain the best talent and resist the toughest economic times because they have a clear reason to survive. The second question is: How is your

company doing what it has set out to do? This is the macro picture, which shows precisely how company resources are leveraged to provide value to clients. The last and final question of the Golden Circle is: What is the company doing? This is an attempt to understand the product or service that the organisation has created to address its customers' needs and, ultimately, realise the organisation's long-term vision. Asking these three questions is a powerful way to frame your understanding of the organisation. Interestingly enough why, how and what is the same sequence of questions that our brains use when they encounter something new and need to understand how to react to it.

Allow me to cite one example of an organisation that is taking the right approach to self-definition. One global IT organisation wrote a document called 'Vision 2020', which became an important part of their recruiting process. The document was a crisp summary of how the organisation related to the three key players in their corporate strategy: their employees, their clients and the company itself. In every sentence of the document, it was transparent that the company was driving to be the market leader; it wanted to do more than increase revenue: it wanted to be one of the best employers in the world and a powerhouse brand. The CEO's words near the end of the document were memorised by sales managers and used in candidate interviews to good effect: "We will be," he said, "a preeminent organisation reaching *every* client, in *every* region, *every* time". Since they wrote the document and started using it for recruiting purposes, the organisation has seen a measurable spike in recruiting success.

I cannot stress enough how important it is to do this prep work before the candidate walks in the door. It makes the first few minutes of the interview easy to manage, and it gives you ready-to-hand answers for the questions that candidates usually ask. Skip this preparatory work and you might get caught flat-footed, which will force you to improvise.

Defining the role

Just as we need to know all of a product's features and capabilities if we hope to sell that product to a customer, we need to understand exactly what makes the organisation a good employer if we are to sell it to the candidate; just as we need to be sure that there is a good match between the customer and the product, we also need to make sure that there is a good match between the candidate and the organisation. We'll look at matching the candidate's needs to those of the organisation in the chapter on the second interview; for now I want to focus on the organisation's needs: these need to be precisely defined before the interviews can begin in earnest.

By defining as precisely as possible the role that the candidate will be filling, you'll be able to provide the precise kind of clarity that the candidate is seeking. Again, you might have done all the prep work you will need here when you were writing your job description, but, depending on how much time has passed between writing the description and the first interviews, you'll want to review the role's expectations, duties, etc. This will help you avoid many of the hiring mistakes that are the result of a lack of clarity on the part of the employer as to the role's expectations and responsibilities. Clarity is, after all, a reflection of preparation.

I once worked for a European IT security organisation. They received an injection of capital from a group of VCs, and one of the group's requirements was that the organisation sustained a growth trajectory that could make it ready for an IPO within four years. The excitement went to their heads and they acted impulsively – and without the kind of objective analysis I've been advocating in this chapter. They decided that, to meet the investors' targets, the sales team would need to be doubled. The problem was that they didn't think about what kind of professional they needed to fill the role before they started aggressively recruiting. It became clear (though not soon enough) that the niche industry in which the company was operating just didn't provide a large enough portfolio of senior candidates to fill the organisation's needs. As they began interviewing these junior candidates, they saw that none of them would be able to deliver the kind of results the organisation needed if it was to adhere to the steep growth curve set by the stakeholders. By the time the organisation decided to focus on training and channel strategy rather than hiring, they had wasted a full quarter.

This organisation should have been thinking about whether or not to add personnel before writing the JD, but, for whatever reason, this step is one that gets skipped. When you're defining the role in preparation for the interviews, double check to make sure that adding personnel is the best route for your organisation. Whenever possible, research some of the other options (freelancing, remote employees, digital marketing, lead generation as a service, etc.) before you start interviewing candidates.

Make sure to talk to your sales leaders to get further clarity about what they're looking for. Combine their suggestions with your own criteria. If it's an inside sales position you're filling, you'll probably want to look for a fairly young and tech-savvy executive – a self-starter with verve and drive. If it's lead generation that you're looking for – whether from a sales development rep, a lead generator, or an opener – you'll probably be looking for resilience, energy, competitiveness and an ability to think on one's feet. Field sales, which covers business development managers, account managers, client execs and client directors, with all their hunting and farming responsibilities, will need to possess a strong executive presence, high levels of enthusiasm, resilience and assertiveness. The more you know about the role and what its expectations will be, the more you can narrow down the list of candidates and the clearer you can be with candidates, when you meet with them face to face, about what kinds of qualities they'll need to possess.

Remember that you'll want to look at how the role will affect the organisation directly (measurables) and indirectly (immeasurables). To guide you during this preparatory work, I've provided a list of questions which should help you further define the role (and therefore your expectations as well):

- How will the role contribute to the company's overarching strategy?
- How will the role contribute to the manager's success?
- How will the role generate revenue?

- What are the skills that are absolute must-haves (e.g. multiple languages, technical skills with certification, legal skills)?
- What are the good-to-have skills?
- How will the role affect the existing team (e.g. new energy, increased competitiveness, new skills)?
- What is the timeframe within which the candidate will be expected to perform (i.e. what is their time to productivity)?
- How much time do I have to fill the position?
- What kind of references will the candidate need to provide?
- What kind of experience will the role demand?

The more of these questions we ask ourselves before we begin interviewing, the more productive those interviews will be. When we have clarity about our organisation and its needs, we can, in turn, provide clarity for the candidate, and that clarity paves the way so that the rest of the interviews can go as smoothly as possible.

CHAPTER 9:
INTERVIEWING (THE FIRST INTERVIEW)
STEP 2: YOU NOW

With our preparatory work behind us, we're finally ready to sit down with the candidate. Once you've made it through the obligatory introductions, during which you'll want to describe the organisation and its need – this should be relatively easy if you've followed the step-by-step process up to this point – you'll be ready to let the candidate start to introduce him or herself. This brings us to the next step in the five-step process: You Now.

Before we dive in, I want to mention one issue that interviewers encounter quite frequently. The truth is many candidates lack clear ideas about their sales skills; even worse, a great deal of candidates are unsure about what they want to accomplish in the long term (a lack of short-term goals is even more problematic, but it's also much less common). We'll explore this issue more when we turn to the next step, You Tomorrow, but it's something to keep an eye out for right from the start. When a candidate's answers to direct questions are vague or uncertain, press for more detail. If they can't provide any, that should tell you a great deal about whether or not they should move deeper into the recruitment funnel. In order to prevent wasted time (yours and the candidates), it's wise to make sure that the candidate is applying for the right job and for the right reasons. You Now will help you do just this.

You Now

This step in the Angle Recruiting Method is one that all interviewers attempt – but with varying degrees of success. The goal of this step is to learn as much as we can about the candidate. What makes them tick? What motivates them? What desirable (or undesirable) qualities do they possess? Don't leap ahead to questions about their long-term goals yet – that'll come soon. First, we need to identify them as they are today and what has made them that way.

Every experienced sales manager has a list of traits that they look for in candidates. Some prefer integrity and respect to intelligence and problem-solving skills; others prefer courage and a can-do attitude to discipline and attention to detail; still others prefer coachability to confidence. Undoubtedly, there will be traits that the specific role you're filling demands – traits that might be a boon in one role might be a hindrance in another. There are, however, a small handful of traits that we can look for in any candidate that will be successful – no matter what their position.

I call these traits the Big Four. They are:

1. Clear purpose
2. Clock speed
3. Curiosity
4. Competitiveness

By focusing on the Big Four, we can free up the bandwidth we need to find the best possible candidate. Without limiting ourselves in this way, interviews can go on for what seems like an eternity. In this chapter, we'll analyse each of the Big Four and discuss how best to measure each of them during the interview.

Number 1: clear purpose

A sense of purpose is the feeling that there is a reason behind everything we do. I've long been told that not everyone has a sense of purpose and that when we find somebody who does have it that should instantly raise that person in our esteem. Conventional wisdom says that when we are interviewing for a position, a sense of purpose should be one of the qualities that immediately move a candidate deeper into the funnel.

Though I, too, place a high value on a sense of purpose, I want to challenge the conventional wisdom, which demands that a sense of purpose becomes apparent the moment you dig beneath the superficial. Our actions are guided by our key beliefs. Imprinted on our young minds and then enforced over time, these key beliefs (about ourselves and others) are at the base of hair-trigger reactions like fight or flight, and we can depend on them to make us act in certain predictable ways. For some individuals, key beliefs dog-pile one upon the other until the individual's true sense of purpose is relegated to the bottom of their hearts where it is almost impossible to reach. If stimulated and nurtured, this sense of purpose will always come out, like the scream of a bungee jumper when the elastic reaches its limit.

A friend of mine has nursed a deep passion for sports cars since he was a teenager. He grew up in a middle-class family, and every evening before supper he would pore over glossy sports car magazines. He found the elegant yet bold lines of Ferraris particularly appealing, and he dreamed of one day owning and driving one. His old man would regularly remind him that Ferraris are reserved for the extraordinarily wealthy and that, with his middle-class background, he would never be able to afford one. He should, his father said, stop wasting time with frivolous daydreams.

Those words left a deep imprint on his psyche. They produced a powerful emotional reaction. He had deep within him a voice that told him he must prove his father wrong. He worked harder than many are capable of for years until, while still in his twenties, he was able to afford the Ferrari he'd long dreamt of owning. At last count, he owns four Ferraris (along with a number of other beautiful exotic supercars).

What was it that made my friend so successful? Was it an undying love of Ferraris? No, it was the determination (deeper by far than his love of a particular sports car) to prove his father wrong. He was driven to success by his deep urge to push beyond—against all the odds—the comfortable mediocrity that had been held out to him as his lot in life.

This power is in all of us. Absolutely everybody, with the right level of coaching, resources and time, can achieve their heart's desire – so long as they want to. These last six words make all the difference. That said, there are many limiting beliefs to overcome and, if we want the recruiting process to come to an end at some point, we need to be able to select a candidate with the kind of drive that will propel them to excel in their position, which means we need to be able to locate this sense of purpose (even if it's buried) during the first interview.

How do we do this? Past performance will guide us towards the candidate's sense of purpose, but past performance is only a partial indicator of future performance. To unearth the candidate's true sense of purpose, we need to understand how they are being driven by their key beliefs. This will give us both the map and the compass that the candidate is using to find their way.

After explaining to them what we'll be doing during the first interview (and why), I warn candidates that some of my questions might touch very personal aspects of their lives. I tell them that, if at any time they feel uncomfortable, they are free to stop the conversation or change the subject.

I've provided a list of questions below that will help you uncover the candidate's sense of purpose. It's highly unlikely you'll need to use all of them. Rather than moving through the list quickly, take the time to explore revealing answers by asking follow-up questions that probe yet further.

1. If money were no object, what would you do with your time?
2. What have you enjoyed most about your past work experiences?
3. Why do you do what you do?
4. What in your life brings you the most joy?
5. What in your life frightens you the most?
6. If you could change anything in your life, what would it be? Why?
7. How do you define success?
8. Which of your accomplishments are you most proud of?
9. If you didn't have this interview today, what would you have done?
10. How would you like to be remembered?

Once we've identified and briefly explored the candidate's key beliefs, it's fairly easy to transition to a conversation about role models (in fact, role models often come up during conversations about key beliefs). Where people draw their role models from can be highly revealing. For some people, they will name people they've never met (business icons, famous historical figures or celebrities); for others, they can be more personal (teachers, family members or close friends); for still others, there might not be a role model at all.

What is important in the conversation about role models is not *who* the candidate has picked as their role model but *why* they have done so. What are the specific qualities that made that person in particular rise above the crowd for them? Here are a few questions to help you guide this conversation:

- What did your role model do to inspire you?
- (If their role model is somebody they've never met) If you had the opportunity to meet your role model, what would you say to them?
- (If their role model is somebody they know quite well) If I were to meet your role model and ask them about you, what do you think they would say?
- What do you think motivates your role model?

I've found that when I open up about my own role model, this puts candidates at their ease, and they feel more comfortable talking about their own role models. I do this when I introduce the topic of role models, and invariably it makes the conversation livelier when it is the candidate's turn to speak. I frequently tell candidates about my grandfather – particularly about his attitude towards life. He made some very difficult decisions during his life, including the decision to move himself and his entire family to a new continent. Through struggles and success, his attitude remained the same.

Though I never met him, I listened when I was a child to stories told about him by his family and the friends who knew him well. These stories inspired me to be the man I am today. My willingness to start a business, my desire to be a leader and an influencer, all of it stems from the feelings I got listening to stories about this great man. I wanted nothing more than to inspire the same kind of respect that is so transparent whenever my father talks about Nonno, when we look through old photo albums, or when I hold his business card in my hands.

One further tool to help uncover a sense of purpose in candidates is a conversation surrounding pain and pleasure – particularly what in the candidate's experience gives them the most pleasure and what the most pain. The seeking of one and the avoidance of the other can be powerful motivators.

The first time I focused on these two feelings, it was truly a revelation. I realised that what causes me pain is seeing people wasting their time and skills working for the wrong companies or in the wrong positions; what brings me pleasure is helping others to be successful. This realisation led me to take the first steps on the path I am walking today.

Since pain and pleasure are the main stakeholders in our decisions, I recommend that interviewers ask candidates what is behind their desire to find a new job. Are they pursuing the pleasure that will come with a fulfilling role in a new organisation or are they fleeing the pain associated with their last position? Their answer to this question will reveal a great deal about which of these two powerful motivators most drives them. It will also tell you quite a bit about how they will deal with adversity when it comes.

Number 2: clock speed

In every environment we find people who somehow always manage to get away with things that, for most of us, would be completely off limits. Think of the classmate who always managed to be ready for the interrogation, or of the university peer who was chummy with the lecturer and ended up with a high grade on his finals, even though you were certain he would fail.

Now think of your work environment. Chances are there are a few people who consistently manage to read the business context, to get promoted, to have more meaningful interactions with senior management, and to make more money than everybody else. In most competitive environments, there are people who are better equipped or better prepared to fight their way to success.

This has been very evident to me since my young days when I was skating at competitive level. I was winning regional championships, which meant I was regularly competing at the national level. At these competitions, I would always see the same face. He and I would compare times, and it was clear that if you put us head to head, I would almost certainly beat him in a 200-metre heat. The thing is, the heats were always composed of groups of skaters, and his fighting attitude always found him leading the pack. What's more, since skaters naturally bunch into groups, he always seemed to know which group would be the one that would make the successful push for the lead at the end of the race.

I've seen the same thing in the world of business – and especially in sales. Some people simply 'get it' faster than others. Others lag behind. If you've been a sales manager for a while, you've doubtless experienced the blank look from an interviewee who has lost the thread.

I call this extra gear that the true competitor has 'clockspeed'. The word actually refers to the speed at which a computer's processor handles inputs. The human brain, while still far more powerful than anything science has come up with (at least so far), processes complex inputs at a more pedestrian pace – but with far less predictable, and therefore more interesting, results. Some people seem, especially when the pressure is on, to respond to multiple stimuli so quickly that they seem to be running at clockspeed. They seem to be able to make lightning-fast observations, taking in everything around them with ease: body language; other non-verbal cues; the immediate environment; tone, rhythm and volume of voice; conversation patterns; all of it. More importantly, they not only observe, they react.

What I'm describing isn't impulsiveness—far from it. It's not even inspiration. It's measured action, but the measurement happens so quickly that it's almost imperceptible. Spotting the right level of clockspeed is as important as spotting the right level of sense of purpose. Like a sense of purpose, the more clockspeed the candidate has the better. This doesn't mean that a candidate that processes information in the midrange of the clockspeed spectrum should be shown the door; it will depend on the role that you are looking to fill (which might suit computations that are more precise than they are fast). That said, sales as a profession does demand a certain degree of clockspeed, and those in the bottom of the clockspeed spectrum will struggle mightily. Though the candidate may have other great traits that will make them successful in life, they probably won't make a great salesperson.

Testing for clockspeed

While other Big Four traits have tests that we need to apply on their own and at specific moments in the interview, testing for clockspeed is something that's done throughout both interviews. It might become apparent immediately, or it might reveal itself in smaller ways. Either way, it's something to look for and, when you see it, take notes about what brought it on (was it pressure, a change in posture on your part, a particular line of questioning?) The same goes for slow clockspeed. When you notice a dip in processing speed – especially if the candidate has otherwise been performing strongly throughout the interview – make careful note of what caused the slowdown.

Since clockspeed is something that, in most cases, can't be called up at will, you'll need to stimulate the candidate in the right way if you want to test for clockspeed. Here are a few ways we can do this.

Pattern of conversation:

During interviews, I make sure to draw frameworks and patterns for the candidate to pick up. I occasionally purposefully contradict myself to see if candidates pick up on and challenge the contradiction (a good sign of clockspeed). If they miss this opportunity, I challenge candidates by asking them if they understand what we are doing and why we are doing it. Many of them will nod, but with their questions or responses they betray, at best, a poor understanding of the exercise's rationale. If they are being overly polite (thinking it will be embarrassing for me if they raise the contradiction), they will often admit as much when I challenge them.

Try setting some basic assumptions. For example:

- I mention at the beginning of the interview that we are in a sales conversation: I am selling the organisation as a solution; the candidate is selling himself as a solution. The sharpest candidates will remember this and will therefore structure the conversation accordingly. Other candidates will quickly drop this structure almost immediately, forgetting that the exercise is supposed to be about demonstrating good consultative sales skills.
- When I introduce the Angle Framework at the beginning of the interview, most candidates show that they understand what we are doing and why, usually by taking the lead in the conversation and following the framework. Some candidates, finding themselves in unfamiliar territory, will struggle. How they react in these moments is very telling. Candidates with poor clockspeed will plough ahead (often in the wrong direction) without seeking clarification. It's like being in a sales call in which you don't understand what the client is saying. A salesperson with excellent clockspeed will recognise

that the conversation is going nowhere and that it's necessary to seek clarification from the client. Those with poor clockspeed will (in interviews and sales calls) not seek clarification even when it is needed.

- Often, if the candidate's performance is lagging during the interview, I will tell them, "Sell, don't tell" or "Wrong assumptions are the major reason why sales don't go through". I'm looking to see if they can apply the insights contained in these to the interview. If the candidate doesn't adjust their strategy accordingly or start asking clarifying questions, this is a big red flag – it tells me that the candidate will dominate sales conversations with monologue rather than listening carefully to what the customer is saying. I am most impressed when candidates try to put themselves in my shoes (it shows they will be able to do the same with customers). They should be looking to validate their assumptions before moving forward to the next step – even if they have to be gently reminded to do so. Unfortunately, many candidates let this chance pass them by.

Progress checks

One of the best ways to test for clockspeed is to stop the interview periodically to ask them how they feel the interview is going.

By asking this question and listening carefully to the candidate's response, we are testing a number of things: the candidate's business acumen, his gut feelings, his emotional intelligence, and his level of empathy. A high degree of clockspeed is often at the root of these desirable qualities. They show an ability to read between the lines and to put oneself in another's shoes. The higher one's degree of empathy and emotional intelligence, the more they will inspire trust (often almost immediately). It makes one highly sensitive to inflection, body language, and other nuanced non-verbal cues. By asking how the candidate thinks the interview is going, you are giving them the chance to showcase these abilities. I've had extremely high clockspeed candidates walk me step by step through each stage of the interview up to that point, telling me exactly when and how they reached me with a particular response or question.

In order to make absolutely sure that I give candidates this test/opportunity, I often make a point of asking the candidate how they think they are performing at the midway point in the interview. Candidates with good clockspeed will take this opportunity to show how well they have understood each exercise that we have done together, recollecting breakthroughs and other points; they will also ask for confirmation *after* they have expressed an opinion (not before). Candidates with poor clockspeed will often say little more than they feel the interview is going well – they won't provide evidence and they won't seek confirmation (though they might try to get me to answer the question for them).

I became aware of the power of this simple question when I was a candidate myself. As part of the interviewing process, I had been asked to prepare a presentation that would sell myself as the organisation's solution. I spent so much time preparing the presentation that I forgot to set a clear agenda for the meeting. Thirty minutes into my presentation, the most senior person in the room interrupted me: "Fulvio, how do you think the interview is going?" I had been so wrapped up in giving the presentation that I had not taken my audience's temperature. When I tried to recover, he interrupted again: "Son," he said," if you continue this way, we will not hire you. Now, close the laptop, forget about the presentation, and restart the entire interview from the beginning." He saved the interview by making me reflect on the interview and my performance in it. Even if the interview isn't going well, this kind of interruption can be a turning point.

A variation of this technique is to drop a bomb in the second half of the interview. Say, "You might not be the right candidate for the role." If the candidate is performing poorly, this won't come as any surprise, but if they are performing well, it will probably elicit a strong reaction. It's testing for interest in the role, clockspeed, resilience, and competitiveness and, as a slightly more aggressive form of progress checking, the candidate's response should tell you a great deal. Ideally, the candidate should ask why he or she is not suited for the role. Again, we're looking for somebody who avoids assumptions and seeks clarity. Right candidates are eager to succeed in interviews, but, when they are failing, they are also eager to understand what they've done wrong.

Number 3: curiosity

Among the Big Four, curiosity is probably the easiest trait to spot in candidates. It's also a very important trait that we want to select for – its absence should definitely not go unnoticed. In this section, we'll discuss the importance of curiosity in a business context, but we'll also look at some of the frequent mistakes that interviewers make when they are looking for curious candidates.

The most basic assumption about curious people is that they are curious at all times and in all places. Curiosity can be broad or narrow. It can lead to intense study in a particular field of interest, to world travel, or to countless evenings spent between the pages of books. While a candidate may not be curious about the interview process, they might be curious about the art of sales, about your clients, your market or your company. This kind of curiosity, even if not immediately apparent, can translate to a long and rewarding career in sales.

In most sales roles, there is the almost-constant need to modify our approach until we have settled on something that produces the best results. Confidence in a particular method is often short lived; the impermanent nature of the market will almost certainly disrupt our modus operandi and send us back to the drawing board. This is where curiosity comes in: it constantly feeds new energy into the cycle, helping us explore the world of knowledge and learn new things.

In my early days after university, I decided I wanted to pursue a job in sales. I spent hours on end at the library, devouring everything I could get my hands on related to sales methodology, the world of sales, how to negotiate, how to communicate and so on. The most successful account executives I knew all read books voraciously, watched YouTube videos and Ted Talks, and listened to podcasts on the art of sales. Some of them had an MBA, some of them didn't, but the latter treated the world of sales as a classroom. It provides endless opportunities to learn and gain hands-on experience (especially when combined with coachability). Valuable business lessons are everywhere if you are curious enough to look for them.

The question remains: what can we do during the interview to gauge how curious the candidate is?

The first opportunity that we have to test our candidate for curiosity is when we meet them for the first time. While an inquisitive candidate is a good sign, better yet is the candidate who has already, in at least a partial way, satisfied their curiosity. The ideal candidate will have checked your social media profiles and they will know about your career and your core skills. They also will have done a good deal of research into your company and its market niche.

If it's not immediately apparent that they've done this research, I like to ask a simple question: How much do you know about our company? A detailed answer is good, but one that shows a clear understanding of the need that the role they are applying for will satisfy is much better. I had one candidate who knew my organisation so well I had to check my notes to provide some of his technical (and apropos) questions. I had another who had reached out to people in my network. He knew far more than my social media profiles revealed, so he was able to ask me questions that I was entirely unprepared for. I had to admire this level of curiosity and preparation.

If a candidate hasn't prepared in an in-depth way for the interview, this isn't grounds to end the interview, but it is definitely a warning sign that should not be ignored.

Active listening skills

Active listening skills are a by-product of curiosity. By actively listening, a candidate shows that they seek clarity and, more importantly, that they know how to get it. We want candidates who, when they offer follow-up questions, it is clear that the question isn't merely a rephrasing of the original question. Active listening is not the ability to string question after question together; it's the ability to hear responses and respond to them in ways that show they've understood them.

I find it disconcerting when candidates start an interview by talking for as long as they can until they are interrupted. You often have to wait for them to take a breath to get a word in edgewise. I am much more impressed by those who combine listening skills with the ability to ask on-point questions and, as a result, speak with authority and clarity.

Homework quality

Later on, we'll be looking at some of the homework we can assign to candidates between the first and second interviews. When they submit what they've prepared to you, take a close look at what they've put together. Has the candidate worked through all the tasks you assigned? Have they rushed the job, or have they taken their time and explored the topic with research? One of the tasks I assign is to research a role model, which should include a conversation with the individual. It is often obvious who has understood the true intention of the exercise and who hasn't. Those driven by a natural curiosity are like journalists who probe their subjects until they yield something of interest to their readers. Those who lack this curiosity ask questions that turn over nothing of any interest to anybody.

Quick-start scenario

I often ask candidates what they would do if they were hired in order to have a fast start and accelerate the team's time to revenue. By asking this question, we hope to uncover the thinking process. Some candidates start by guessing that the key to a fast start is going through the training as quickly as possible. Others would turn to their new colleagues for help. The best candidates go straight to the top achievers in the organisation and ask them how they've become successful. The difference is, once again, the level of curiosity. The non-curious candidates expect training and support to give them what they need. The curious ones seek the best possible answer – often the fast track to success.

Before moving on, I want to make a quick note about coachability – which is related to curiosity. Since we want candidates who are prepared to embrace the company culture, we also want candidates who are eager to learn, and this eagerness is a product of curiosity. The curious are always willing to empty their cup of tea so that their cup can be refilled. They are confident but coachable.

Assessing this can be tricky. The best way I have found so far is to role-play a specific sales situation. In the roleplay, I first ask the candidate to play the role of a salesperson trying to sell me a branded pen. Then, we reverse roles. Finally, we reverse roles again, but I ask him to sell the pen in a different way from the way they sold it the first time. This exercise has a way of highlighting problematic attitudes towards coaching. If they are too stubborn to embrace new ways of doing things, they might not be coachable, and I am extremely wary of uncoachable candidates.

The following questions can help you uncover curiosity in a candidate:

- When was the last time you finished a book? What was the book?
- What do you know about our company?
- Do you have any hobbies?
- How do you prepare when you go travelling? Do you read the guidebooks, go with a tour group, or explore on your own?

127

- What was the last skill that you learnt? How long ago was this?
- When you are in the market for a new piece of technology, how do you decide which one is the best for you?

Number 4: competitiveness

Ideal candidates (and ideal salespeople) find the competitive environment that comes with working in sales highly stimulating. It gives them the chance to sharpen their skills every day and offers them constant opportunities to prove themselves. Since salespeople's success is tangible (i.e. measurable) it is easy to compare yourself and your performance to your peers. Even if there's nobody to compare yourself with, you can compete with yourself, using your numbers from last year, last quarter, or last month as your benchmark.

The best candidates are those who aren't remotely satisfied with average or sub-average performance. True competitors are pushed, as though by an invisible force, to climb the ladder and join or even surpass the top performers in the organisation or the industry. If the candidate says that they will be perfectly satisfied with average or sub-average performance, you might want to ask them why they are even considering a career in sales.

I am not saying that you need to be competitive to be a good salesperson – it certainly helps, though. Being a competitive person surrounded by other people with a similar drive to be the best is what makes sales such a fun discipline. Imagine an Olympic sprinter running a race against a group of people who all wanted nothing more than to cross the finishing line without breaking a sweat. What drives the world-class sprinter (and the salesperson) is the desire to be the best against the best that the world has to offer.

Non-competitive people tend to dislike being measured or compared to their peers. This results in a massive blind spot: they can't see (or don't want to see) the size of the gap between them and those they are being measured against. Poor results are too easy to shrug off, and true success will almost always be out of reach.

To a competitive person, poor numbers send a very different message: they are a wake-up call, a leaderboard, a map that shows who is ahead and who is behind and what kind of strides need to be taken if the leader is to be overtaken. Competitive people don't usually get frustrated looking at numbers; they don't have time for useless frustration, and the only thing they care about is working out ways to get 'up there'.

We want employees who are chasing that feeling of fulfilment, but this isn't all. One of my mentors once told me that the easiest path to fulfilment is setting very low expectations. Competitive people set the bar very high. They want to be first in their discipline; second place is just the first loser.

There are a number of reasons why we should want competitive people on our team:

- they are easier to motivate
- they are easier to understand (their behaviours are more predictable)
- they are constantly thinking about ways to improve, to set the bar higher and higher (today's excellence is tomorrow's standard)
- they don't settle for mediocre results
- they tend not to have limiting beliefs.

I've been competing in some form or another for as long as I can remember. When I was a kid it was roller-skating, then rowing, swimming, running, dancing, studying, and, eventually, selling. Like most child competitors, I was motivated when I was young by the desire to please my parents but, as I grew older, I became addicted to the taste of victory.

I remember practising every day, working at my craft, applying the lessons taught to me by my coaches, looking at my competitors and teammates and trying to copy their techniques. When I started my first job in sales, I applied everything I had learnt from years of competition: I would come to the office before anybody else, practise my pitch until I could do it in my sleep, make as many calls as I possibly could, and I would emulate the most successful account executives, trying to make their techniques work for me. The competitive streak in me was the foundation of my success, and today I don't hire anybody who doesn't show at least a glimmer of this trait.

There are many ways to find out if candidates do or do not have this competitive spirit.

Explore the candidate's background

Sports draw competitive spirits, so candidates with backgrounds in sports are usually competitive individuals. I have hired basketball players, runners, football players, swimmers, bodybuilders, triathletes, the list goes on and on. People used to competing have experienced success and failure; they know how to manage the pain that comes with the latter and they thirst for the pleasure that comes with the former. Athletes also know the value of discipline and mental strength (these are as essential as oxygen in sales environments).

131

Remind the candidate that they are in a race

The interview process is (or should be) competitive in itself. If we have done a good job of sourcing candidates, we have more candidates than vacancies. This means that only some of the best people interviewed will make it through to join our company. I like to remind candidates during the interview that there are a number of particularly qualified individuals vying for the positing. If their energy levels dip, they are easily defeated; if their energy levels surge, you've struck a vein of competitiveness.

Challenge the candidate

We discussed this technique in the clockspeed section. What you want to elicit is the 'I'll prove you wrong' reaction. Suggest that you're not sure the candidate has the kinds of qualifications or qualities you're looking for, or explain that the environment is more competitive than they might be prepared for and watch the competitor come to life. If the candidate gets excited and starts questioning you to understand how wide the gap is between them and the other members of the team, that's a very good sign. Such candidates are not only fighting back (a sign that they're not easily defeated), they're also showing a willingness to learn exactly what it takes to be the best in the organisation.

Those with a great deal of fight in them can be great candidates (so long as they're coachable).

Ask for the 'brag file'

Braggadocio isn't appropriate in every culture, so some candidates will downplay their skills and abilities. Break through this by asking about their achievements. I like to call this the 'brag file', and it's often the best way to see how successful and competitive a person has been in the past. Ask them to send a file containing all their achievements, awards and successes. A consistent track record of overachievement is a sure sign of a competitive (and therefore desirable) candidate.

Increased focus on inclusiveness has led to questions about the kinds of limits that should be placed around competition. The most frequent critique of competition is that it might be detrimental to team spirit and cooperation. The answer to these critiques is simple: as long as your team members have integrity, there can never be enough healthy competition. The combination of honesty and competitiveness produces world-beating performance.

Issues arise when organisations hire individuals with low levels of integrity and emotional intelligence. These problems can escalate when episodes that demonstrate a lack of integrity are left unaddressed. There is a difference between healthy competition and dog-eat-dog, and by focusing on results over integrity, you'll end up with the latter.

Here's a list of questions that will help you uncover competitiveness:

- When was the last time you had to compete for something? How did the competition make you feel?
- Do you practise any sports?
- How do you think you're different from the other candidates?
- What would you be willing to sacrifice to be successful?
- What would you not be willing to sacrifice for success?
- Looking back at the last time you failed to succeed, what could you have done differently that would have led to a different result?
- How did you feel when you won your last deal? Did the feeling last some time or was it short lived?
- What's your key to achieve success?
- What's your stretch goal?

To find candidates with all of the Big Four is no easy task. I often focus a little more on clockspeed and clear purpose than on curiosity and competitiveness during the interviews.

You can always uncover and stimulate the latter two during the probation period. That said, it's not uncommon that a particular line of questioning uncovers all four of these highly desirable traits in a candidate, and we should always be aiming to attract and hire sales people with such a highly desirable blend of traits. If you don't find a candidate with the qualities you're looking for, keep looking. Top organisations don't become so by settling for mediocre talent; they rise to the top by exclusively searching for and hiring outstanding talent.

CHAPTER 10:
INTERVIEWING
(THE FIRST INTERVIEW)
STEP 3: YOU TOMORROW

Now that you've identified the candidate's You Now (focusing on the Big Four desirable traits we discussed in the last chapter), it's time to look more closely at the candidate's angle as it compares to that of the organisation. Again, we want to find significant overlap between the candidate's personal journey and the organisation's vision for the future. We call the stage where we start to examine and compare these angles 'You Tomorrow'.

Over the years, my conversations with candidates have evolved. The more I introduced the topics of goal-setting, dreams and aspirations, the clearer it became to me that understanding the journey that the candidate is on (or wants to be on) is key to the planning and matching that happens later on (we'll turn to both of these soon). Like questions designed to uncover a sense of purpose, questions designed to discover the candidate's angle often turn up something surprising: Many individuals have never really asked themselves what they want to do with their life; it's as though life is a current of coincidences that have merely dragged them along.

Good candidates will speak in clear language about their journey and its trajectory. Discovering their angle should be relatively easy. Less-than-ideal candidates will speak in vague ways about the future. There can be a vision of success, but the milestones between the present and the more-successful future are, at best, murkily defined. Looking into the future is something we've all done at one time or another (hopefully before we've started studying) but, for too many, it's not something that is given the kind of intense concentration and focus that it takes to make a vision concrete. A goal is not enough. Without understanding that it is not just the destination but the trajectory as well that must enter into this thought process, significant progress towards that goal is unlikely.

This is one of the main reasons why so many people end up stuck in a life that they hate – trapped in a golden cage. They haven't taken the time to think deeply about what steps they need to take to achieve their goals. As time passes and their goals still haven't been realised, they tend to revise their goals downwards. Though they might end up with a financially rewarding career, they can still feel as though they've been living somebody else's dreams.

When we have the luxury of more candidates than positions, we must reject candidates who have not thought their career through. That said, Angle Recruiting gives the interviewer the opportunity to challenge the candidate to think about their career in ways they might not have previously. This is what makes Angle Recruiting such a powerful tool for those looking to hire young professionals.

When I first started designing the Angle Framework, issues surrounding this planning were some of the first I encountered. When I was conducting trials, I first tried a 10-year plan, but there were too many unknown (and unknowable) variables in a timeframe that wide. I then tried a three-year plan but, though it made establishing milestones much easier, the timeframe was too narrow. In the research that Daniel Gilbert did to prepare for his book, *Stumbling on Happiness,* he found that people dramatically overestimate what they can do in one year but they highly underestimate what they can do in 10 years. I decided to strike a balance between these two by using a five-year plan in the Angle Framework, and it almost immediately struck a chord. After a number of trials, it became clear that a five-year plan is short enough to plan precisely but long enough to broaden the horizon of possibilities.

The four scenarios

Candidates may not have a precise vision of what they want to achieve in five years, but the right approach and the right questions can trigger emotional responses and gut reactions that will give us a rough idea of what the candidate's angle is. The further we press for clarity, the clearer the angle becomes. I've found the best way to begin this process is to offer the candidate the following four scenarios:

- Scenario #1 (the entrepreneur): Without entering into too many details, the entrepreneur scenario is characterised by not having a direct manager, having the ability to decide the direction of your business, but with responsibility and no regular income.
- Scenario #2 (the corporate executive): You have grown through the ranks to occupy a senior position in the organisation. You probably have a team of people reporting to you. Your management tells you the direction that the company is taking, and you can only partially influence these decisions. You have a regular income and benefits.
- Scenario #3 (family first): You are a loving and caring parent who devotes your time to your family. Your partner is the 'bread winner'; you ensure that the family life runs smoothly.

- Scenario #4 (the globe trotter): You are a philanthropist who travels the world to discover new cultures. You are financed by NGOs and, to make extra income, you write articles.

I ask the candidate to take a deep breath and choose the scenario that makes the most sense to them. We're looking for a strong emotional reaction to one of these, and this reaction should guide you towards some follow-up questions. The first of these is perhaps the most obvious: Why? The answer should give you some idea what motivates the candidate and how much they have thought about their future.

At this moment in the interview, it's important to let the conversation flow naturally – you'll also want to take notes throughout the talk. You'll find the following questions (grouped according to their appropriate scenario) good ways to guide the conversation:

Scenario #1:
- What kind of business would you be running?
- Would you be running the business on your own or with partners?
- What resources do you have already?
- What will you need to realise this vision?
- How will this business influence your family,

friends, your clients, your employees and, more broadly, the world?

- What will your (and the organisation's) legacy be?

Scenario #2:

- What specific role are you filling in the organisation?
- Is the role in sales or outside of sales?
- Are you managing a team?
- How will you support people working with you and for you?
- Are there any particular organisations you would be proud to work for?
- How would you define success in this role?
- How much would you like to earn at the peak of your career?

Scenarios #3 and #4:

- If this is your dream, why haven't you done this already?
- How would you feel you are contributing to society?
- In what ways would working for this organisation enter into this scenario?
- What would bring you the most fulfilment in this scenario?

The questions for scenarios one and two are designed to elicit clear thinking (and clear answers) about career goals and aspirations. As you would have noticed, scenarios three and four are tricky ones. People who choose these scenarios are usually on the verge of a major life change, and you'll want to ask straightforward questions at this point to quality the candidate for a long-term position in sales.

Closing the interview

You should be at the point now where you can wrap up the first interview. By now, with the help of the Angle Framework, you should have a clear picture of the candidate and whether they are a good fit with the organisation and should therefore be moved deeper into the recruiting funnel. To close the interviewyou should therefore get them to summarise their understanding of how your organisation will help them to achieve their personal and professional goals.

This is another great moment to test for clockspeed. Ideal candidates will show that they have understood the process and will have gleaned important organisation-specific information that they can then use to make a strong closing argument. This argument should use evidence from throughout the interview that proves that the candidate is a good fit for the organisation and vice versa.

If you are quite certain the client will be moving on to the second interview, assign two pieces of homework. These will help them plan for the next interview and think through the process they have experienced.

Homework: vision boarding and vision confirmation

This will help candidates think about their goals (mid-term and long-term) and focus on the direction that they want their lives to take. During the interviews, the talk about goals and aspirations may have been improvised. If the answers you get in the homework aren't identical to the ones that they provided in the interview, that should raise an eyebrow, but it might mean that the candidate, after careful consideration, changed their mind.

I assign two pieces of homework for them to complete before the second interview. The first is a vision board. Vision boarding features prominently in Joyce Schwarz's book, *The Vision Board,* and has been a staple in motivational circles for some time. We can vision board by hand or we can do it electronically. A vision board contains images, words, and anything else that specifically relates to a hoped-for future moment in time. I usually ask candidates to include things that illustrate their expected lifestyle (house, car, etc.), their family, friends, their job, and anything else that is relevant and meaningful. The goal is to help them define their vision and focus their energy on attaining it.

Since sales people are a visual bunch, they often find the exercise motivating and even fun. I also recommend sharing the vision board with family and friends to receive their inputs. Modern technology allows you to create a vision board in a matter of minutes, and the results can be not only revealing but visually appealing as well.

The second piece of homework is a vision confirmation. This is about checking the assumptions that are an inevitable part of our vision. The life of an entrepreneur or executive is not always what people think it will be. This can lead to visions that are poor reflections of reality (be particularly wary of candidates who place a great deal of emphasis in their vision boards on the lifestyles of the wealthy).Let's say that the candidate imagines being the regional vice president of a software company in five years. They may think that this will be a fulfilling and rewarding role, but they need to confirm this. To do this, they could contact a regional vice president and ask him or her about how rewarding and fulfilling the role is. They might be surprised by the answer, or they might have their vision confirmed in every way. Encourage candidates to delve as deeply as they can when doing their vision confirmation. Have them ask about both the positives and the negatives. What do they love about the job and what do they find difficult to cope with? Ask them if they could change one thing what it would be. Finally, be sure, at the end of the interview, to ask if there's anything else they want to share.

CHAPTER 11:
INTERVIEWING
(THE SECOND INTERVIEW)
STEP 4: PLANNING

The second interview should begin with a homework review. Reviewing the candidate's vision board with them is an excellent way to check for (and challenge them on) consistency. Let's say that during the You Now stage of the interview, we made note of a clear sense of purpose linked to family values. Perhaps the role model was a senior member of the family who created a prosperous family business. When we review the vision board, we should expect to find images of families (perhaps the candidate's own), a picture of the role model or something connected with the family business.

Reviewing the vision board allows us to drill deeper, to access the candidate's core values and sense of purpose. Assuming that they were selected carefully, the words and images on the vision board should add depth and breadth to our mind's-eye portrait of the candidate. If the vision board is visually dominated with luxury goods, it's fair to assume that the vision lacks field depth (it's questionable, if any serious reflection has gone into vision boards, if they focus solely on the material trappings of success). We're looking for stretch goals, not fantasies.

Once we have reviewed the vision board and mutually agreed that it's both meaningful and feasible, we can move to the second part of the homework: the vision confirmation review. Between the first and second interviews, our candidate should have located and interviewed somebody in the same kind of position they are angling for. If they couldn't get ahold of anybody to interview, that should ring alarm bells. If they're applying for a sales position, prospecting skills are an absolute must, and that's essentially what they're doing when they're looking for interview candidates.

The focus of the vision confirmation should be, not the agreements, but the discrepancies between the candidate's initial assumptions and the real-to-life picture that the contact provided. I have been particularly impressed by candidates who came to the second interview and were willing to admit that their assumptions didn't withstand vision confirmation. For some of them this resulted in a very different (but more realistic) vision for their future. At the very least, you should see that candidates have made adjustments (large or small) to their timeframe that reflect what they have learned in the vision confirmation process.

Planning

Now we turn to building a mutual plan, one that includes both the candidate and the organisation and will help both achieve their goals. During the first meeting we identified these goals. It's now time to work with our candidate to help them get where they want to go. This planning stage is one of the ways that the Angle Framework really separates itself from other approaches to the interview process. I have found that a relatively small investment of time during this stage pays sizable dividends down the road.

We say that a journey of a thousand miles starts with a single step. This is the idea that we want our candidate to understand. It doesn't matter how big the candidate's goals are. What is fundamental is that they identify the first few steps that will start them on the path to their fulfilment. Too many people make great plans, but, frightened to take that first all-important step, they never follow through on them.

Working at the planning stage with candidates often leads to breakthroughs, and these breakthroughs need to be seized upon, they need to be turned to actionable ideas as quickly as possible. American researchers recently found that good ideas that are not acted upon quickly fade into the background (with many people, this happens within as little as five seconds). What we want from our candidates is mental action; we want them to turn breakthroughs into possibilities and possibilities into opportunities. We want them to leave the second interview feeling that anything is possible and that our organisation is the ideal place for them to pursue their goals.

Planning requires a few standard components that we can help the candidate take note of:

- Resources availability: People tend to underestimate the resources available to them. Thinking with an open mind about resources that might be used to further their ends with the organisation will open up unexpected opportunities.
- Ideas: These can be discussed when going over the entrepreneur scenario as well. Talking about the candidate's entrepreneurial ideas (especially when they relate directly or indirectly to the organisation) is a great way to start planning for the future with a candidate. An open conversation can also help candidates clarify their business ideas, both for themselves and for you.

149

- Budget: How much will the candidate need to earn and save if they are to be able to achieve their vision?
- Skills needed: Candidates need to be aware of the skills they will need if they are to realise their vision. During the interviews, it's worth highlighting the fact that skills are something that the hiring company will be able to provide and improve.
- Network needed: Who in the candidate's network can help him or her to realise their vision? This is another area where you'll want to highlight the organisation's ability to help the candidate. By leveraging their daily sales activities, they should be able to expand their relevant network.
- Building good working habits: Sales is one of the best professions for people who want to sharpen their business habits, climb the corporate ladder, or start a new business. Attitude and behaviour should, therefore, be a major focus of the hiring process.
- Personal brand: Everything candidates do to create their unique personal brand helps attract business opportunities and adds to the organisation's brand and credibility in the industry. You'll want to stress the fact that a strong personal brand is the result of outstanding performance, a world-beating attitude, and exemplary behaviour.

During the planning stage of the Angle Framework, we have the opportunity to test how candidates plan ahead to achieve their goals. Also, we are able to experience first hand what it is like to work with the candidate on business initiatives. Most importantly, it gives us a chance to look at the candidate's angle in detail. Each milestone the candidate adds brings their angle into focus, and we can assess how much commonality of intent there is between the candidate and the organisation.

If the candidate is successful, they will be accountable; they will be expected to actualise the plans they made during the interviews – to realise the vision discussed in the interview phase. Since we don't limit goals and aspirations to the business arena, some of these plans might not involve the organisation. It is good, however, to be aware of all the candidate's plans— even those we don't have a stake in—as these may directly or indirectly affect the candidate's future relationship with the organisation. It may prepare us for the day when the candidate will leave the organisation, perhaps to change career streams or to focus on family or other personal goals.

As a performance-driven industry, sales features exceptionally high turnover levels. There are lifelong sales executives, but it is helpful to remember that those we hire today are likely to move on to other pastures at some point in their careers; this might be within the same company, or it might not. A good sales manager focuses on retaining highly motivated sales executives for a minimum of two or three years. Anything more than that should be considered a blessing. This makes succession a must. If we work with candidates from the outset to help them plan their future(and build their trust in the process), we can be in a position to drive or at least influence the succession process when it happens.

CHAPTER 12:
INTERVIEWING
(THE SECOND INTERVIEW)
STEP 5: MATCHING

We've reached the final step in the interviewing process. We have introduced our organisation, its core values and strategic goals that management hopes it will achieve within the next five years. We have introduced the role as well, showing exactly how it supports the organisation's goals (and hopefully those of the candidate too). We have tested the candidate for the Big Four traits, and we have helped them to visualise the future and then confirm this vision. Now that we understand their personal and professional goals, we can plot their angle and determine where the candidate's and the organisation's journeys overlap.

As tempting as it might be at this stage to continue to sell the organisation, we have to let the candidate take the wheel at this point. Let them drive the conversation. Before we do so, however, we need to provide some guidance. We need to let the candidate know that we'll be looking for (and expecting)four things:

- We need them to summarise the journey that we have been through. The candidate needs to show that they are clear not only on *what* steps have been taken but *why*. In a sales environment, this ability to summarise will serve them well when they are at the tail end of a complex sales cycle. This will also help us further confirm clockspeed, curiosity and coachability.

- We need them to provide clarity on anything that the interview process might have glossed over or missed. We've come to the end of the interview process, and now is our chance to go over our notes and seek clarification. The candidate should continue to impress during these moments of clarification. This is when we can clear away any negative gut reactions we might have had at any point through the process. If, when we push the candidate in one of these areas, they respond in a way that confirms our gut feeling, this is our chance to push further and either resolve or confirm our doubts.

- We need them to explain precisely how our organisation will support the achievement of their personal goals. This is where we start to match the candidate's angle with the organisation's angle. Since the candidate should be in the driver's seat at this point, it's good to allow them to start this matching process without being led by the nose into it.

- We need them to recognise that it's closing time. Let's never forget that we are in a sales environment. The candidate should still be selling him or herself as a solution to the organisation's needs, and (if the interview has gone extremely well up to this point) they should also recognise that this is the time to make a strong closing argument. If, when you leave the door open for them to do so, they don't show that killer instinct, this might be reason enough to reconsider the candidate's fitness for the role.

Wrapping things up

During this last stage of the interviewing process, we need to remain as unbiased and analytical as possible in our assessments of the candidate's answers.

A few important points to highlight:

At this stage, it should be clear to both parties why it's worth trusting each other and why keeping anything concealed does a disservice to both parties and the organisation. Throughout the Angle Framework, we have built trust and rapport to the point that there should be almost no chance that a lack of integrity will cause everything we have built together to break apart. The process—from first step to last—is designed to build a degree of trust and openness that should continue between the interviewer and the interviewee long after they have joined the organisation.

As the interview draws near its close, propose one final roleplay during which the candidate can display their abilities. This will allow us to understand how mature the candidate is and how much energy and time we'll have to invest to bring the new hire to the minimum level they'll need to perform at to be a productive member of the team.

The roleplay will need to go through the following sales skills:

- opening
- selling
- handling objections
- closing.

The opening will help us to understand the candidate's interpersonal skills and style. Selling will show us what the candidate knows about sales methodology and if his selling style flows naturally or is something of a bumpy ride over long lists of features. Objection handling is yet another test of clockspeed, and it shows how they operate under pressure. Finally, closing shows us the candidate's teeth; we want to see how good he is going to be at getting fish in the boat. As Alec Baldwin's character in *Glengarry Glen Ross* would say, all that matters is that the client signs on the line which is dotted.

If you haven't had anybody else participate in the interview process, this role-playing is a good chance to do so. Our opinions, once formed, are difficult to break through; we tend to see only that which validates our recently formed notions, so fresh pairs of eyes and ears are assets. They might pick up something important that we've missed. Whenever possible, try to involve members of the team, and be sure to encourage conversation between the candidate and these team members. You can observe for active listening and interpersonal skills, and the candidate can get a second perspective of the organisation.

Also remember that this is closing time for us as well. If the candidate has expressed any doubts about the organisation or management, this is your chance to clarify and, if you feel ready to do so, you can explicitly offer them the role. If they are a good closer, the candidate might also ask for confirmation and for the contract. The general assumption in this case is that we interview salespeople and we expect salespeople to strike great-quality deals when the iron is hot. I've made selecting a candidate part of the final step because it's always wise to consider candidates in an objective and detached way, so, if you're not ready, don't offer them the position. If, however, you are certain that the candidate is a perfect fit for the organisation, it's perfectly reasonable to jump the gun.

We want to make sure we close the interview on a high note and ask for feedback on the overall process – even asking for ways to improve the process. This is not only done out of politeness, but out of curiosity. The more we know about how the candidate feels at the end of the process, the more we can hone the method to a fine point. Over the last few years (and especially since I founded Fellettis), I have been driven by the Kaizen concept, which seeks overall improvement through small and measurable changes at the micro level. By improving service, quality, technology, processes, company culture, productivity, safety and leadership, we improve the organisation as a whole. The Angle Framework is no different. Its rules are not carved in stone. Each of its facets might be improved, and candidate feedback will make sure this improvement happens.

The Angle Framework as a life tool

Before we move on to the onboarding process, I want to take this moment to look back at the Angle Framework and examine it, as it were, from a different angle. When I first started applying the Angle Framework in my professional life, the responses I got often exceeded expectations. Candidates were not only clearer about the role they would be filling and the organisation they would be joining, but they were also clearer about their purpose in life, about their goals and their aspirations. I have since learned to see the Angle Framework as a powerful self-improvement tool, and I encourage you to use it in this way.

Many of my clients have reached out to me during times of intense life change. Some of these changes were for the good, but many of them were not; many of my clients came to me when they were in the midst of turmoil and happiness seemed to be beyond their grasp. For the last few generations (the baby boomers or Gen Xers) happiness meant something very different. If you had asked our parents to create a vision board, they would likely have put a nice school or college for their kids, a secure job, a healthy and happy family, a nice house with a garden, a car big enough for the whole family to ride in, and perhaps a pet. This kind of life would have satisfied that generation.

159

Today, happiness is less of a tangible thing. Today's Generation Y and tomorrow's Generation Z have learned to think critically about material rewards and their relationship to happiness. The experience-based economy shows us daily just how widespread this has become. Globally, many millions of us are on journeys to fulfilment very different from the ones our parents walked, but many of us are lost, unsure of where to turn. This is why so many of my clients come to me with the same question: "How can I be happy?"

To those who feel as though they have lost their direction, the world of motivation offers its balm. Motivational books and seminars each promise the path to a happier and more fulfilled life, but too many of those who read these books and go to these seminars are paralysed, convinced that the search for wisdom and self-knowledge (not the same thing) will one day lead them to the happiness and fulfilment they seek—and it might. Other people reach out to life coaches or psychologists who can help them understand the inner workings of their own minds. Still others plunge into the world of transcendental meditation or world travel in search of their deepest and truest selves.

When you feel as though you lack direction or purpose or as though happiness is out of reach, doing something is definitely better than not taking any action. But the world is beset with inactivity. There are untold millions of people who, instead of attempting to fix their problems, decide to hide at home in the darkness, watching TV and waiting for the hours to tick by. There is so much waste of human potential!

My theory is that people in many parts of the world have been raised with beliefs that, in a different context, would have prepared them for a successful life. Let me give you a real-life example:

Roberto was born in Italy in the seventies. He grew up with the belief that earning a technical degree was his ticket to a good job, a comfortable income, and the opportunity to build a family. When he was awarded his degree he found a good job working for a large multinational. Everything went smoothly until the multinational decided to reorganise and move his department abroad.

Roberto grew up believing that his happiness was directly related to the country he lived in (its familiar customs, faces, and places). His life was comfortable, prosperous, and happy, but if he wanted to keep his role with the organisation, he had to move abroad. Roberto, like anybody who considers relocation, thought about the many challenges ahead. The life he had prepared to live was suddenly no longer available to him. It was as though he had readied himself for a long road-trip from Rome to London. In the glove box was the map of Europe with all the stopping points clearly marked. Just before the journey was to begin, though, he was suddenly transported (car and all) into the middle of the Arizona desert. The roadmap was still there, but it no longer corresponded to what he could see out of his windshield. The engine was running, and the destination was the same – how to get there was a different matter.

When I met Roberto, he was still sitting in the middle of that desert in a car idling in neutral. He was paralysed, unable to act decisively. He was working as a security guard at a warehouse, and he was, to put it mildly, dissatisfied. Long overtime hours and nightshifts had robbed him of his motivation; his health had taken a turn for the worse; he knew the life he was leading wasn't sustainable, so he came to me for help.

Our first major breakthrough came when we started looking at his angle, at how his current trajectory didn't remotely align with his goals. He had a choice: either revise his aspirations downwards or re-angle in a way that would see him moving, once again, towards a fulfilling and prosperous future. To do the latter, he needed to break out of his narrow comfort zone.

We took a close look at his deepest personal and professional aspirations, and it became clear that what Roberto wanted was to be an internationally recognised photographer. He had a skill gap that needed to be closed for this to be attainable, and he also needed to be willing to travel extensively if he was to build an international reputation. We used the Angle Framework to examine his present and his future, and to establish milestones. Once the path was clear, the first step became easier (and far less daunting).

Roberto lives in Bulgaria now, where he works for an international modelling agency. He is building a reputation, and his goals seem more attainable then ever. He and I both credit the Angle Framework for some of his success. His talent and drive deserve the lion's share of the credit, but it was the Angle Framework that provided him with the clarity in terms of vision and trajectory that he needed to take that first step. The Angle Framework is a powerful tool when it is used in this way. It helps us to recognise when our trajectory loops back on itself rather than moving onward and upward. It helps us see when we are standing in our own way and limiting our own possibilities.

CHAPTER 13:

SELECTING AND ONBOARDING

Now that you've reached the end of the interviewing process, you should have a candidate who is eager to join the organisation and become a productive member of the team. What's more, if you followed each of the steps along the way, you should be able to predict at least relatively accurately how successful they will be. Again, this is not an exact science, but the more you apply the method, the more you'll see how it adds to your ability to assess and predict accurately.

Whenever I reach the end of a successful interview process, I feel so overwhelmingly energised. I've found a new star (or, even better, new stars) to add to my team. Before I add anybody, though, I like to spend some time on the selection process.

The first thing I like to do is get a second (or third) opinion. I usually involve a small handful of other people in the interviews, and I like to sit down with them when I've narrowed the field down to a few candidates and get their unfiltered take on each of them. There are often small things I didn't notice during the interviews that are brought up during these conversations. They might challenge my gut feelings, or they might confirm them. Though we want to explore our gut reactions (and those of your colleagues who also met the candidate), the goal here is to put our heads together in order that the selection can be as objective as possible.

If a clear winner doesn't emerge from this process, I like to schedule a phone call with each of the remaining candidates. Since these calls are often the result of lingering doubts, I tell the candidates why I am hesitating to offer them the position. I then give them the chance to prove that they are, indeed, the candidate I should be hiring. Just like earlier in the selection process, I occasionally have a second party listen in on the call to see if my doubts are justified. After the conversation with the candidate has ended, the second party and I compare notes and discuss our gut reactions to the conversations with the remaining candidates. This is usually enough for me to make a final decision.

Once you have decided who you will and who you won't be hiring, finish the selection process by calling the candidates to tell them what your decision is. If you want the interviews to be a powerful tool for rejected and accepted candidates alike, provide ample detail when you tell candidates your decision. For successful candidates, tell them exactly why you have awarded them the position. For unsuccessful ones, be equally clear. World-class recruiters don't let HR deliver bad news for them, and they are upfront and transparent about their reasons for hiring or not hiring an individual.

Once the candidate has accepted your offer, it's good practice to follow up with an email that goes through the following points:

- Areas of excellence: Highlight the areas in which the candidate overachieved during the interviews. Try to eschew subjective opinions in favour of fact-based feedback that the candidate can use to guide them toward best practices and build confidence in their early days with the organisation.
- Plan and match: Outline the information that was covered during the planning and matchings stages of the interviews. Touch on why the relationship will work and what roles the new employee will need to fill so that the organisation and the individual can both achieve their goals.

- Areas of improvement: This is also the time to highlight any of the gaps that the interviews might have uncovered. Whenever possible, outline what you'll be doing and what the candidate should be doing to address these issues in the coming weeks and months.
- Expectations: Provide clear expectations, but also be sure to highlight what the new employee can expect of you (and of the organisation). Show them how you will be there to support their journey.

In the days before the official start date, you'll want to keep open communication channels between you and the new employee. Provide them with material to read and perhaps some motivational readings and, of course, copy them in on the most important team emails that you send out.

You may also want to organise a team lunch to introduce the new hire to the team the week before their official first day. During the same week, you'll want to make sure that all administrative aspects (email address and other key applications) are taken care of. Workspaces, laptops, desktops and mobile phones should be ready to be handed over on the hire's first day. I also like to prepare a new starter guide, which outlines the new employee's priorities for the first few weeks or months. It's good as well to include as advisers all people (AEs, product managers, etc.) who will be involved in the training and the onboarding phase. The more stakeholders you involve in the onboarding process, the faster you can expect the new hire to become productive.

Different organisations approach the first day differently, but there are a few things that I've found ease the onboarding process significantly. First of all, and perhaps most importantly, the hiring manager should be present for the new employee's first day. When they arrive, invite the new hire for breakfast and have a 30-minute welcome chat. During this chat you will want to provide what I call an 'inoculationshot'. This is simply a reminder that new employees who surround themselves with positive people who show a can-do attitude and don't accept excuses or limitations will significantly increase their chances of success. In every organisation, there are people with very different states of mind, moods and energy levels. Some are optimists, others pessimists. By choosing carefully who they surround themselves with, new hires set the tone for their experience with the organisation. It's important to give the inoculation shot on the first day. This tends to make decisions about who to associate with conscious ones.

On the first day, it's also important to remind the new employee exactly what will be expected of them, how they will be measured, and what the organisation will need to see before they can be promoted. When I talk about promotion with new hires, I usually focus on three metrics:

- Attitude: A positive attitude is an absolute must. People in the team need to be able to see the glass half full all the times. We all have challenging moments, but people with a positive attitude quickly deal with them and move on without wasting time.
- Behaviour: People need to be ready to collaborate, share, support and inspire others. If you can't (or are unwilling to) do these things, you're simply not doing your job. Single-minded focus on personal goals is impressive, but cooperation and collaboration should be viewed as something that contributes to these personal goals.
- Performance: Deliver on your commitments. By doing so, you will realise your personal goals and help the organisation to reach its goals as well. You have to be accountable and responsible for doing your part – just as your manager is responsible for creating the environment in which you can overachieve.

From the first day, it must be clear that failing to live up to these expectations has consequences. There is a flip side that should also be made clear from the outset: there are resources available that will help the employee meet management's expectations; training, coaching and support will combine to make even high expectations attainable.

Every sales team that I build adheres to the same basic principle: every member of the team is an entrepreneur that runs a franchise. The company provide each member of the team with training, a salary, a selling territory, facilities and infrastructure. As with every business, the entrepreneur is responsible for the results. It is their responsibility to use the available resources so that the business can continue to grow and prosper.

Over the years, I have run dozens of onboarding meetings. With the improved interviews that the Angle Framework make possible, combined with a great onboarding experience, the chances of success improve dramatically, as does sales productivity in terms of time to revenue.

CHAPTER 14:
FINDING TIME TO ANGLE EFFECTIVELY

In a sales manager's week, there are so many tasks and responsibilities, and so many of them are deemed urgent – everything is a top priority. I remember in my early days, just after being promoted, my inbox was suddenly overflowing. I was receiving three times more correspondence than I had been before being promoted. This, I found, is just part of the sales management territory.

Management is asking you for mandatory meetings, your people want to involve you in deals, not to mention forecasting, reports, approvals, and training new hires. The demands on your time might seem endless, and with so much on your plate, it might be tempting to relegate recruitment and the interviewing of candidates to, at best, secondary importance. Recruiting only becomes a priority when there is an urgent need to hire extra sales staff.

The reality is that if you wait until a need arises to start recruiting people, you will have to wait several weeks (if not months) before you fill the position. If the need is the result of the acquisition of a new, important client who needs account management, the pressures will start to mount while you are looking for a suitable candidate. As the leader, you will probably have to step in and cover for the missing sales rep. This will only make finding a suitable candidate more difficult, and it means that you're even more likely to settle for a candidate who is, at best, partially qualified.

Here's what happens when you run the sales team in a small company without strong recruitment practices:

An event triggers the need for an extra sales rep in your team. It can be attrition, growth, relocation, or anything else. The clock starts ticking:

- You have to think about precisely what kind of sales rep you need (hunter or farmer, with experience or to be groomed).
- You need to check how much is in the budget for new hires.
- You have to prepare an effective JD that will allow you to attract good-quality candidates.

- You contact agencies and brief them on your requirements.
- After a couple of weeks, you start receiving the first candidates.
- Two weeks pass before you find someone suitable for the position.
- Finally, you can offer the role to the candidate and prepare the contract.
- In a lot of cases, good candidates are still attached to their previous employer. They need to submit notice to their employer, meaning they aren't available to start for another month at least.

Best-case scenario, it takes two months from the time you realise you need an extra body to the time when you fill the position. During this time, you'll need to keep the sales machine running (effectively covering for the new employee).

This is what happens unless you develop a habit of regularly interviewing people.

Effective recruiting practices will vary depending on the size of the organisation:

- In smaller organisations and start-ups, bandwidth is limited, so we probably won't be able to spare more than a couple of hours a week to interview new candidates.

- In medium-sized organisations with more than one sales manager, we'll be able to split recruiting and interviewing tasks among the team, which means that there should be about one half-day per week spent interviewing in the organisation.
- In larger organisations with an internal recruitment team, the time spent interviewing can climb all the way to a couple of days per week.

Don't wait until an issue rears its head to start interviewing. You should *always* be interviewing. If you don't have an opening, you should make that clear to candidates, but you should still be scanning the market for potential candidates to put on your bench – you nurture these candidates just like you would long-term clients. Considering the liquidity and the competitiveness of the job market, you cannot afford to wait.

Even when we are at full speed, with our processes running smoothly and our management style polished and effective, there are situations that we cannot control. Family relocation, illness and accident, just to mention a few, can strike at any time and we must be prepared for it if we are to avoid losing time and revenue.

Once we decide to reserve time out of every week to meet new candidates, we need to be sure that we use this time wisely. Not including prep time, Angle Recruiting should translate to about three hours spent with each candidate. The time is split as follows:

First 90-minute meeting:
- Setting the context
- Introducing your company DNA
- You Now
- You Tomorrow
- Assign homework

Second 90-minute meeting:
- Reviewing homework
- Planning
- Role Play
- Match

Some people have also found success by having three interviews (each of them one an hour long). This stretches the process out a little longer, but it also can avoid the dips in energy that might come with longer meetings.

It's important that you set clear checkpoints at every stage along the way. As you approach these checkpoints, you can check to make sure that the candidate is comfortable with the process (and that you are happy with the candidate's progress). If both you and the candidate are uncomfortable, you might be able to save each other more wasted time. Do not fall into the politeness trap. If you feel like your time is being wasted (or like you're wasting the candidate's time), don't be afraid to speak up. Grimacing your way through an awkward and time-wasting interview isn't in anybody's best interest. When I'm meeting a candidate who clearly doesn't meet the criteria I've established, I give them no more than 20 minutes of my time before ending the interview (abruptly if necessary).

Time is a limited commodity that we need to protect at all costs. By recruiting and interviewing regularly, we can make powerful use of a relatively small investment of time. Powerful recruiting strategies will allow us to reap the many benefits that being present in the job market affords us. We'll be attuned to shifts in the talent pool, and we'll have a stable of winners ready to step in when the circumstances call for them to do so.

CHAPTER 15:
ANGLING TO RETAIN TALENT

I have been privileged to work for global organisations that have developed and encouraged a culture of retaining and fostering talent over decades. Later in my career, when I started working with small and medium IT vendors and coaching start-ups, I realised that something that seemed to come naturally to the larger organisations was a concept completely unknown (or thought of as purely academic) in smaller organisations.

It's no mystery that when you operate a start-up, you are spread thin; you need to produce enough to manage cash flow, and to do so seems to take all of your energy, which means that talent management is little more than an afterthought.

I've seen talent management from all positions in large enterprises, but it's much more rare in SMEs and start-ups. The small organisations and the large ones that are thriving understand the importance of powerful recruiting strategies. They know that not investing in talent management practices can result in lost revenue, profits and cash flow.

The impact of poor hiring decisions, as well as that of losing key members of your team, can reach dramatic levels. This is especially true in sales environments, where not keeping senior people motivated and satisfied with the organisation can have substantial bottom-line impacts.

As an example, let's consider a senior sales executive with a seven-figure portfolio. If you lose them, not only are you losing years of valuable experience, you're also losing a crucial link to your most valued clients as well as the potential business they were on the verge of bringing in. The situation can become even more drastic if the same rep goes to the competition. You're handing your advantage to your competition, which can double or treble the already sizable impact of the departing employee.

This is why I encourage my clients (and you, my readers) to use Angle Recruiting as a way to retain your key personnel. We've already discussed how it can be used to locate, assess, and hire talented new staff, but you can also use it to protect what you have already built. In order to retain talent, you need to empower deserving individuals organisation wide. Promotions need to be possible, so the organisation will also need to be on a growth trajectory. There needs to be an investment in employee skills, so there needs to be scholarships and other upskilling resources. There's also a growing movement towards corporate social responsibility, which can foster intense employee and customer loyalty.

For each of these to be effective, we need to understand our employees. We need to know what motivates them, how they challenge themselves, what their long-term goals are, and what they need if they are to feel adequately rewarded. I've mentioned above that in this changing world we can hope to keep our employees highly motivated in the same role for two to three years. Particularly in sales, companies need to have a clear career progression to give employees the opportunity to capitalise on the lessons learnt and take increasingly complex assignments.

This is where the Angle Framework can be of tremendous assistance. We can skip the steps that focus on the organisation and the role (employees should be clear on both of these), but we can use the parts of the Angle Framework that focus on the individual and their goals (You Now, You Tomorrow, Planning and Matching). It boils down to putting a structured mission of discovery in place. This should be applied for each sales rep in your team, and it needs to include follow-up actions and periodic reviews.

The mission of discovery starts with a meeting between the manager and the rep. The focus of this meeting should be a deep and meaningful conversation that focuses on uncovering the rep's sense of purpose, their core beliefs, and their vision for the future. It's important that you keep track of all these missions of discovery and reviews. They should be built into ongoing coaching activity, so they shouldn't become an administrative burden.

When organisations grow, we expect to see the adoption of human capital management solutions, and we may see HR start to take the lead on employee retention programs. Even in these instances, the sales leader needs to keep abreast with the level of symbiosis between his employees and the company. We all know that employees leave managers, not companies. By showing that you understand the employee's priorities (and take actions to ensure that these priorities play a part in your plans for the employee) you will be able to retain employees with ease.

In a survey we recently ran here at Fellettis, we identified that 30 per cent of the respondents felt their manager had a minimal understanding of their needs. In the same survey, we found that the main reason that employees leave an organisation within the first year of joining is the mismatch between expectations set during the interviews and the reality that followed. The second most common reason is a poor relationship with the sales manager.

In establishing reasonable expectations and ensuring that both the employee and the organisation live up to them, sales managers play perhaps the most important role in ensuring that employees are both effective and loyal. Angle Recruiting (and particularly the Angle Framework) makes the manager's leadership role easier and more powerful. It offers sales managers the chance to make individual development conversation more meaningful and forward-looking.

CONCLUSION

For the last 18 years, I have been a participant in and an observer of the world of sales. With each passing day it becomes clearer and clearer to me that companies with powerful and considered recruiting strategies are the ones that are leading the way in terms of growth and performance. Success in sales starts with selecting the right people (and selecting them in the right way) so that they can contribute to the organisation's success. The tools in this book are the product of my experience, and they will, if applied mindfully, help your organisation keep pace with a rapidly changing world.

A changing world makes the tasks of attracting and hiring sales talent more and more difficult, so you need to tailor your approach to today's professionals (especially if it's young professionals that you're looking for) and you need to also make your recruiting strategies channel specific. Angle

Recruiting will help you to address today's best candidates – and in a way that will make sure your JD gets noticed.

Most importantly, Angle Recruiting will build a strong degree of understanding between you and the candidate. It's a method that cuts through the clutter to get to the heart of the matter. By using Angle Recruiting, you'll be sure to find the candidates that are vision-aligned; since their personal goals dovetail neatly with the organisation's vision, they'll support the organisation's growth (just as the organisation will, in turn, support theirs).

I believe that every manager who aspires to be a true leader has the responsibility to support and drive the growth of his or her employees as professionals, but also as individuals. True leaders ultimately enable their employees, helping them to succeed in ways that power the success of the organisation as well. This is why we put the individual at the centre of the recruitment process.

I'll close with a vision: think of a world in which every sales organisation attracts people who passionately add unique value to that organisation and, of course, to its clients as well. Visualise a job market in which every salesperson can achieve his or her personal goals by working for inspiring sales leaders. This is the vision that fuelled the creation of Angle Recruiting, and I hope that every manager reading this book can bring that vision to his or her organisation and to use it to pursue success in powerful and world-altering ways.

ABOUT FELLETTIS

Fellettis is a sales consulting and training company that impacts its clients in three ways:

1. We help our clients attract and hire outstanding sales people.
2. We help our clients retain their top talent.
3. We help our clients to get the most out of their existing staff, making sure their sales teams perform well above industry norms.

With more than 18 years of sales coaching and training experience, I am an entrepreneur and author who is intensely passionate about sales and the ongoing success of my clients. I am proud to say that my team and I have more than a century of cumulative sales experience.

We may not have all the answers (nobody does), but if anybody has the answer, it is us.

Many companies struggling with performance add new employees or spend prodigally on expensive sales training, hoping that one of these solutions (or both of them) will solve their issues. The problem is that they have, in many cases, incorrectly diagnosed the issue – they're applying the balm to the wrong areas. The assumptions that inform these hasty decisions lead to a massive waste of money and resources. Indeed, they often create more problems than they solve.

With this in mind, we have created a five-step delivery methodology:

1. Observe
2. Assess
3. Develop
4. Deliver
5. Coach

In the first two steps, we ask your clients about your strengths and weaknesses, then we analyse the results and prepare a report for you and your leadership team.

In steps three and four, we use our intellectual property as well as our Partner Ecosystem to tailor the best possible training that addresses your specific needs and issues. This training is delivered in an impactful way and, in step five, we reinforce what has been taught through ongoing leadership coaching.

Globally, over 60 per cent of the employed workforce is in a sales or sales-related position. I wake up every morning motivated to positively and profoundly impact this group – I believe that doing so can make the world a better place.